Dirty Luggage

By Rebecca Stone

-1-

Matthew, England 1968

He trailed behind his mother, observing the wiggle of her bottom as it stretched the fabric of her skirt from one hip to the other. Turquoise and brown flowers trembled with the loose wobbling of her thighs. Slightly stooped over the shopping trolley, she concentrated on the list held against the bars in front of her, every so often peering at the overstocked shelves, the packaging garish under the strip lighting of the store.

"Mum." He realised she hadn't heard him, "*Mum.*" He heard the whine in his voice and knew it would annoy her.

She snapped her head round to him, a deep furrow beneath the wiry curls of her fringe "What, Matthew?"

"Can we have spaghetti tonight? Please." Again the whine; he hated himself for it.

She looked at him, his soft brown eyes, appealing to her under the flop of his dark hair. It was the tone of his voice that annoyed, grating on her nerves as it had when he was a toddler, always wanting something, always *needing* something. Even now, with the pot bellied skinny limbed

2 Dirty Luggage

body of a pre-pubescent, his unbroken voice transported her back to those early days. Spaghetti was such an easy request to fulfil, there was no reason she couldn't grant it and it would curl the serious boys face into a rare smile. Her brow relaxed and she measured calm onto her face. "Sure honey."

Out in the car park Matt bent at the waist as he manoeuvred the full shopping trolley around the puddles. His mother followed, counting her change and scanning the receipt as she fiddled with the zip on her purse. The sky was overcast, an ominous weight in the clouds threatening to squeeze its contents on to their heads. June Isaacs looked down to the soft, white doughy loaf sitting on the top of one of the carrier bags. "Quick Matthew, hurry up."

As they loaded the crinkly white bags into the boot of the Morris Minor, huge plops of rain landed on their heads, it's cold fingers spreading across their scalps. Matt shuddered, beginning to feel damp and uncomfortable. He sprinted across the car park with the trolley, every so often jumping on it, leaning his weight over the bars until he sent it wheeling into the trolley bay, enjoying the crash as it hurtled into the others.

3 Dirty Luggage

He hopped into the passenger seat, the stale smell of cigarettes and powdered ash-trays enveloping him, ruffling his mop of hair he covered the glove box with wet droplets.

"For God's sake Matthew, you're like an old dog."

He leant across to the radio, twisting the dial 'Jumpin' Jack Flash' filled the car. June made a loud, exasperated sigh. "I don't know how you can listen to that racket."

"It's number one Mum," Matt grinned as he looked out of the side window, watching other shoppers, heads down over their trolleys, scurrying like wet rats to their cars.

"Come *on* Matthew." His mother called from underneath the lid of the boot as she hoisted bags onto her arms, the handles cutting off the circulation leaving red bangles along her forearms. He swung his legs out of the fuggy warmth and padded to join her. "Here, you can manage these." She passed him two bags which he hooked into the centre of each palm. He followed her up the narrow concrete path of the front garden, heavy tins banging annoyingly into the sides of his legs. His mum was busy pressing the doorbell, heaving the loaded weight of her arm up to the buzzer. "Come on Barry," she growled. "Where are you?" She was peering through the bevelled glass window, looking for the heavy shadow of her husband as he approached the door. Instead she was greeted with the light empty space of the hallway that led to the kitchen windows. The house appeared empty and cold, the swish of cars on the main road and the plopping of water collecting and streaming down the guttering the only sounds that filled Matt's consciousness.

He placed his bags on the path, it was slippery with the rain that had soaked into the mould and algae, like sponges they filled up, the path becoming a dangerous slide from the front door to the street. He submitted to the rain that now streamed under the collar of his football shirt, his nose now running with the cold. The snot tickled as it crept out from the warmth of his nostrils.

"Stop snivelling" his mother snapped and Matt wiped his nose with the back of his hand, the snot tightening the skin before morphing into the same slippery substance as the path.

Finally, she let the bags slip off her arms and pulled her handbag from round her back. Her white, fat fingers rummaged through old tissues, sweet wrappers, tubes of crimson and fuchsia lipsticks, a hairbrush covered in long blonde strands, a crumpled silver packet of Lambert & Butler cigarettes and a fake gold lighter until, with a reassuring jangle, she found the keys to the house. They traipsed the bags through to the kitchen, setting them down on the lino tiled floor.

"Can I go now?"

"Just play in your room, dinner will be ready soon"

Matt trotted back down the hallway towards the front door before turning and racing up the narrow staircase, two at a time. His eyes were focused on the dark pink carpet, the shag worn, an almost bare path leading to each of the three bedrooms and into the bathroom at the top of the stairs. His bedroom was at the front of the house, over the front door, a small box room adjacent to his parents. He twisted his feet at the top of the landing and pointed them towards his door, how many strides could he make it to his room in? Fists clenched, belly button sucked into his spine he stretched his front leg out, toes pointing for every extra inch of ground cover, he could see the pink of his big toe through the weave of his Argyll socks, a Christmas present from Nan. He felt a soft bump into his forehead. He raised his eyes and found himself looking at a foot covered in a dark blue, slightly shiny sock. As he straightened his neck he could see another socked foot dangling beside his head on the other side. His breath caught in his throat and his heart began to pound in painful lumps in his chest. His spine uncurled as his eyes followed the contours of the feet to where they joined the bottom of a pair of brown trousers, cheap polyester the perma crease flattening at the knees. He took an unsteady step backwards. The thin belt of the trousers was hidden by the soft, rolling stomach. The fabric of the white cotton vest so thin the dark cavern of the belly button was a shadow. Slowly his senses now picked up on the smell. It hung, pungent and warm in the air, a putrefying sweetness to it. Matt started to gag. His hand instinctively flew to his mouth, clamping down on the cold, sweaty skin. He allowed his eyes to continue their slow, torturous journey upwards. A chin rested on the neck of the t-shirt, lips purple and swollen, glistening with spittle, surrounding a mouth hanging open. There was something pink and round filling the mouth, like a huge berry lodged, too big to swallow. The realisation that it was a tongue slowly dawned on Matt, it looked as if you could chew on it. Thin strands of black hair hung straight down like tassels from a curtain and underneath, the terrifying, blank, monstrous stare of his father. Forever staring at a patch of the carpet beneath him. A grotesque puppet he hung from electrical cable that had been slung round the loft ladder that was sitting, like a bridge, across the hatch.

Matt opened his mouth to scream, almost stuck together, his lips parted slowly. A hoarse whisper was all that escaped. He tried again, still no use, like a serpent a dry rasping that cracked in his throat. He started to walk backwards, holding on to the banister, he slid each foot down the wall of the steps. He couldn't pull his eyes from his father. He now had a side view. His head hanging onto his chest as his neck was held upwards.

Finally he reached the bottom of the stairs, turning he saw his mothers legs from under the open door of the fridge, a shopping bag at her feet. He walked slowly towards her and tugged the fabric of her skirt.

"What is it?" another tug "Matthew, I'm busy, what do you want?" she leaned backwards and around the door. Her mouth remained open, ready for the next admonishment but on seeing the pale, waxy face of her nine year old boy, the words faltered.

"What's the matter?" Matt's mouth was also still slightly ajar but still the words would not escape. June bent down, eye to eye with him. "What's the matter?" Matt looked away from her towards the staircase, a small, trembling finger pointed upstairs. June pushed Matt to one side and walked down the hallway, her heavy frame pounding up the staircase. He gazed blankly through the window of the backdoor, his brain vibrating with each of his mothers' footsteps. Halfway up the stamping stopped. Her scream startled the neighbour's cat sitting on the fence at the back of the garden, it's fur

9 Dirty Luggage

bristled as if electrified, it's bottom raised to the sky as it tipped itself off into the back alleyway.

His desk was at the front of the class, wooden with an old-fashioned ink holder and a table top that opened to store exercise books. The teacher's back was turned as she wrote lines of speech across the board, chalk dust floating to the floor in soft, powdery mists. Matt held the compass in his right hand, each time a flicker of his father's face crossed his mind he would stick the sharp point into the palm of his left. He tried to focus on Miss's words but they could not penetrate the bubble that had formed around him, distorting sound and detaching him from the classroom. She turned to face the class and instructed them to pick up their pencils and copy the lines from the board, adding the correct punctuation. Matt closed the compass and held it tightly in his left hand, the cold metal hard in his fist. His right hand held his pencil, it hovered over the blank page of his book. The fine blue lines seemed to rise from the page, begging to be pinned down with writing. They began to swim before his eyes as the tears pooled in the corners. He screwed his eyelids shut, maybe if he kept them closed, just peered at his page through the smallest gap, he could stop his father's face appearing. But he couldn't close his nostrils and the smell kept haunting him. Like nothing he had ever experienced before, why had his father smelt like that? His dad had never smelt good, sweat and stale beer, but he'd been able to talk himself into accepting that as the smell of man. As identifiable as the coffee and cigarettes that clung to the breath of his mother. This new dad horrified him. He had talked to him throughout the night, Matt hadn't been able to understand him, the fat, swollen tongue making his words indecipherable. The dribble kept running from the corners of his purple lips, the front of the cotton vest becoming darker as the pool of spittle spread . The first notes of the dawn chorus broke the spell, releasing Matt from the nightmarish clutches of his father's spirit. The winter's morning was dark and he had stayed in bed until all the shadows in his room had disappeared, he couldn't bring himself to open the door of his bedroom. A physical barrier, it marked the space between the sanctuary of his bedroom and the landing where he had convinced himself the ghost of his father still hung. His mother was too busy to notice, she had been on the telephone as soon as it was reasonable to expect other people to be awake. He had crept past their bedroom door, hoping for the gruff sound of his father's voice to interject with his mothers shrill tones. Finally, he lightly ran through the space that his father had occupied the afternoon before and flew into the bathroom, slamming the door behind him. He stood at the toilet bowl, a clash of avocado against the sickly pink carpet. He angled himself unusually, so that he wouldn't have his back to the door. A loud rap made him jump, interrupting the stream of his pee.

"Are you ready for school?" it was his mother.

"Not yet Mum." Surely he didn't have to go today?

"Well, get a move on. You'll be late." She kept her voice level, there was no need to disrupt Matt's routine. It would be the best thing for him to be with his classmates and away from the home for the day.

And so Matt struggled to pull himself back to the classroom. He looked up from his desk to the board again and noticed Miss looking at him. She gave him a small smile, a tiny sign that told him she knew. She was pretty. She always wore soft sweaters over skirts that closed in at her knees, showing the sheer, silky tights that slid smoothly into her tiny heeled shoes. When she walked past his desk a waft of fruity shampoo and flowery perfume lingered after her. His heart ached and pulled towards her retreating warmth, he just wanted to be held for a little while.

At playtime Matt lingered in the classroom. He hadn't told anyone yet and wasn't ready to speak the words. No-one had actually told him what his father had done. He had seen his father in the loft before but the ladder was always there. He would use a pole to hook it out and then it would come sliding down in two stages. Matt thought it was magic and couldn't wait 'til he was old enough to be trusted to do it himself. Instead he would have the job of standing on the bottom rung while his dad creaked his way up and into the hatch.

Once all the other kids had left the room, Matt slowly walked out to the playground. He moved imperceptibly along a low brick wall and sat at the end. Branches from a dense and straggly bush planted above, concealed him in their foliage.

June sat at her dressing table. 'It', was now three days ago and she needed life to return to normal, the usual routines, as if nothing had ever happened. She picked up her wooden hairbrush and weaved her fingers through the bristles collecting a small nest of hair. She placed the soft ball onto the table and marvelled at how it didn't simply float away but propped itself against the blue pot of her Nivea cream. She backcombed and hair sprayed until the bleached bob rose from her scalp in what, she hoped, was an illusion of volume. Holding her powder compact in one hand, the soft pad in the other, she looked to the mirror, the first time she had properly studied herself since 'it' happened. She was convinced there were new lines creasing the skin underneath her eyes, thinner too, a faint shadow underneath her cheek bones. There was a flicker of movement at her bedroom door. Through the mirror she could see the figure of her son standing at the doorway, he seemed smaller than usual. She wondered how long he had been there? It gave her the heeby jeebies him watching her like that.

"You need to get ready for bed Matthew. Go clean your teeth and get your pyjamas on. School tomorrow."

She continued getting ready for work, applying her make-up, creating a bar-maid's mask, concealing the strain of the last few days. She heard the flush of the bathroom toilet and the light flutter of Matthew's feet as he ran along the hallway to his bedroom. When had he got so light on his feet? She continued getting ready; slowly. Hopefully, by the time she was dressed he would have fallen asleep. She squeezed her feet into a pair of worn, black court shoes, smoothing out the

15 Dirty Luggage

folds of her stockings that wrinkled above the leather encasing her ankles, and crept to Matthew's door.

Sticking her head into the bedroom she caught a waft of Shalimar, what on earth had the little bastard been doing with her perfume? A shaft of light from the hallway fell across his single bed. He was lying rigid, point straight, his blankets pulled up to his nostrils. He certainly wasn't sleeping, his eyes were squeezed shut too tightly. What was going on in his head? She'd be buggered if she knew. That bastard husband of hers; always did have a streak of the duldrums about him, depression they called it, and now he'd screwed them all up, probably messed the boy's head up now as well. Sighing, she sat on the end of Matthew's bed, a small squeak accompanying her bottom as it sank into the old mattress. His body tilted towards her, she could swear there was a trace of a smile on his face, like he's wishing for something nice. Oh well, she couldn't hang around here, she had to get to work, the neighbour would stick her head in the door and check on him.

-2-

Guy, Present Day

Guy Hudson was not the normal prisoner. At thirty-two and with the health of a man who had filled his soul and belly with a life of fresh air, sunshine, seafood and good wine; his energy struggled to contain itself within the unforgiving walls. His floppy, caramel coloured hair fell into a loose wave that gently brushed his prominent cheekbones. Clear blue eyes were set widely above an aristocratic nose, the unbroken bone a clearly defined ridge in the landscape of his tanned face. Full lips rested on near perfect white teeth, a gentle smile that welcomed conversation and laughter, conversation that was difficult to achieve within the confines of the British penal system, and so, with a mind that was clawing for freedom, Guy turned to the library. The weight of the hardbacks resting in his arms induced a little excitement. Pleasure and stimulation had to be found in the most simple things nowadays, the thrill of a new book, allowing his uninspired brain cells to accept education, knowledge, was the most he could hope for. As for conversation, well, that had to be kept for the prison fitness room. He had achieved the position of gym orderly, the most prestigious and respected job to be had, it allowed the prisoner to socialise with the officers that chose to exercise there too. As he raised the books to his nose, inhaling the oily scent of the well thumbed paper, he felt relaxed and, for a little while at least, happy.

"What you got there Captain?" The officer standing at the entrance to the landing, pulled Guy from his reverie.

"Oh I had a bit of luck today. Josie managed to get me a couple of books on vineyards and wines."

The ruddy faced officer broke into a smile, the thick skin on his cheeks creasing, squashing the large pores into slanted specks. "Ah you gonna retire to the South of France then eh? Turn your hand to a different intoxicating substance."

Guy lifted his stomach muscles in his best pretend laugh. "That's right, a legal one this time."

The screw lifted the bunch of keys that were hooked onto his waistband, turning from him to unlock the large metal door that led back to the landing.

"Well, I guess I better let you back to your study then."

18 Dirty Luggage

"Thanks mate."

With relief Guy passed through the door, stepping ever so slightly sideways to avoid brushing the large stomach that claimed the small space. It was association time and several inmates loitered along the landing on the route back to his cell. Some leant against the wall, territorial, casting their eyes over their domain, a psychological jostling to be regarded as a hard bastard. Others rolled from one cell to the next, their drug thirsty eyes cast to the floor in their attempt not to attract attention. Occasionally the hum and waves of conversation would be punctuated with an ape like holler as an inmate cursed the space around them, depression, anger or madness forcing expression through their larynx.

Guy strolled amiably along. A few friendly nods were thrown in his direction. He didn't bother with too many in-house politics, some respected him for it, others envied him and their bitter stares were meant to intimidate. He refused to acknowledge the vibrations from the stream of damaged and dangerous minds, doing his best to look self absorbed until he stepped into the sanctuary of his own space. He threw the

Dirty Luggage

heavy books on to the bottom bunk, it was his study area, the top bunk he saved for sleeping. For the moment he had the six by eight space to himself. A precious time of solitude before a new cellmate would impose all their bad habits, life stories and obsessive routines onto him.

'Hmm, what to do first, read or write?' Guy's internal conversation played itself out on his face as his brows knitted into a question. Looking at the painted brick wall in front of him a photograph caught his attention. A smiling blonde beckoned him to write. 'Ah my darling Gina, are you waiting for a letter? Are you missing me?' He pulled the small, fold up chair to the desk and perched on the hard metal seat. 'But, it is so hard to know what to say, there is bugger all news, same old, same old. Maybe you would like to hear about my new books and I can share a little of my dream with you.' Guy smiled to himself, she may not be the one but she was the only one he had and, so far, she had stuck by him. Bending over his notepad a small stream of sunlight fell from the tiny window' catching the highlights in his hair, the grey of the concrete prison and the small exposure to the white light of England had not yet dulled the warmth that had previously cloaked him.

Gina had sent him a photo that he had taken only two weeks before he was arrested. She was standing on the boat, her muscular legs deep brown against the stark white of her shorts, a loose navy and white stripy sweatshirt falling softly over the contours of her broad shoulders and just hinting at the pert, firm breasts that hid behind the fabric of the top. Guy loved the photo, not for the attractive girl who worshipped him but for the expanse of ocean he could see behind her. That was his real love, the deep blue goddess that rocked him, sometimes rising against him, her power so breathtaking, a challenging, testing relationship that had begun at the age of ten. On his first dinghy the cold, salty air turning his hair crispy and whipping his cheeks red, Guy just wanted to absorb it. Harnessing the power of the wind and riding the jarring bumps of the Atlantic. Closing his eyes he filled his mind with an image of the ocean, it's blue haze as far as the horizon, finding the space in his head that his body ached for.

21 Dirty Luggage

A howling siren cracked the image into pieces, the blue ocean momentarily turning black. His eyelids flicked open quickly as he turned to face the cell door. The siren continued to assault his ears, it's howling wail like an uncomfortable and attention grabbing child. It meant there was trouble somewhere in the prison, more often than not a fight. A nasal voice boomed down the tannoy system;

"Bang up, bang up now!"

Guy strode quickly to his door, flinging the heavy metal shut, the lock engaging with a clunk. He leant against the cool steel, pressing his ear against it. He could hear the heavy footed running of the officers on his wing as they raced along the landing making sure each inmate was securely behind their locked doors.

Bollocks, it was the second Friday of the month as well, his Boef Bourgignon evening. That and a little snifter of bourbon afterwards. In exchange for passing tips from his father's stables one of the screws would bring him his favourite dish from an old mate's restaurant. With a bloody fight to sort out he would be lucky if the bloke could get to his cell tonight. His father had begrudgingly obliged the request on the proviso that Guy would not ask him for any more money. Remembering the visit he found himself smiling. Poor dad, after all these years of cursing his son for his alternative lifestyle choices he then had to come and see him in prison. It was good of him to come really, you could see how uncomfortable he had felt. He was tall and immaculately groomed, his grey hair combed away from his forehead, skin so freshly shaven it looked young and supple. The brushed cotton shirt had a softness, like a cheap studio portrait, the imposing figure was slightly misty at the edges. The brown and red check screamed of the countryside, loudly out of place amongst the town and city families around them. His mum's petite frame was so tightly entwined around his arm that the effect was one of a barnacle clinging onto a large, powerful ship. Guy noted her denim jeans and pale blue shirt, an effort to dress down but with her collar up and her hair loosely coiled into a French pleat, she remained beautiful and elegant. He joined them at the small round table, mum had already covered the formica top with crap food from the snack bar, thin, dark brown coffees sat in wilting cardboard cups. His father was leaning back against the smooth moulded plastic chair, fixed to the ground he could not gain the distance he wanted from the table. His mum stared into his face, the pain in her eyes sent daggers to his heart. Seeing her son in the drab, grey prison clothing had stripped her brave face away. The tears wobbled side to side along the sill of her eyes. Fumbling through her pockets she searched desperately for a tissue.

"Bloody bastards wouldn't let me bring my handbag in here," and she smiled, sending the tears tumbling. They streamed through her make up leaving tracks like rain down a dirty window. His father had adopted his marble expression, like air distorted by heat, the anger seethed from him. Guy slid into the chair closest to his mother, the psychological protection of the table between him and the stern presence opposite. He looked to his mother's watery blue eyes and felt the choking hard pebble in his throat; he didn't trust himself to speak. Her small, cool hand gently brushed his cheek, it said I love you and offered forgiveness. Lying on his bunk, his breath caught as that same hard pebble threatened to burst the dam. He closed his eyes and, like a spectator, tried to relive the visit with emotional detachment.

As he made the request to his father he could see the beseeching in his mother's face, the lines across her forehead and her trembling lower lip begged her husband to help their son. He knew dad's preference would have been to see him rot. "Such a small thing Charles, surely you could?" Her voice had shaken, barely a whisper amidst the loud, emotionally charged atmosphere of the visitors hall. His father surveyed the room, the agitated nerves of the young drug addicts, the roughly shaven, large bodied figures of the career crooks, habitual residents of this dreadful institution, and he knew his son would struggle. "For gods sake Guy, when will this stop, where is it all going to end?"

He felt like a teenager again, it didn't seem to matter how many years passed, his father still managed to strip away his adulthood. The two men stared, their profiles mirroring one another, the strong nose and prominent brow of the Hudson family sliding from one generation to the next. "I don't know Dad." And felt his gaze slipping from the deep brown eyes.

"Look around you, Jesus Christ son, just look at where you are." Aware that his father's strong, upper middle class voice was beginning to attract attention, he was keen to deflate his rising temper. He looked up from the table and into the hawk like face. "I'm sorry, this is the worse it's ever got to and I have absolutely no intention of allowing myself to repeat this experience. It was an idiotic, foolhardy thing to do and I should have known better. Sod's law I would get caught eventually."

His father's large top teeth bit down onto his lower lip as he cursed through a closed mouth "It's not about sod's fucking law is it? It's about your stupid, fucking decision to load your boat up with cannabis."

Trudy lay her hand on top of her husband's. "Please Charles."

A couple on the table beside them had lowered their voices, keen to overhear the conversation of the posh bastards next to them. Trudy could feel the wife's heavily made up eyes boring into her, jealous bitterness drawing hard lines into what could have been a pretty face. Her husband, wearing identical clothes to Guy, curled his lip into a sneer as he grunted conspiratorially to his white blonde wife, the collection of gold chains and crucifixes bouncing on her chest as she laughed.

"You have had every advantage in life, every opportunity to make something of yourself and what path do you choose? Drug dealing, a bloody drug dealer for a son. Think of your poor mother having to come to this godforsaken, hell hole."

"I don't know what to say dad. I cannot defend myself, I know I don't deserve your sympathy, I know I have abused your generosity and I realise that I am asking too much of you now."

"Damn right you are. You're asking me to put my professional reputation on the line. Can you imagine." Charles leant forward across the table, throwing his voice in a whisper "Passing bloody tips into a prison!"

Guy also bent at the waist, bringing his head closer to his fathers. "If I can get on the right side of the officers it could mean that they recommend me for an open prison sooner."

27 Dirty Luggage

He could see his father cracking, the eyes relaxed and lost their severity. Maybe it was for the sake of mum, maybe, just maybe it was a small gesture of love but in the end he agreed. No sooner had the soft moment arrived it disappeared again, making Guy doubt it had ever happened. The next emotion cut him with a coolness he had never felt before. Leaning across the table in the calmest and quietest voice he had used in the whole visit, his father hissed at him "Don't you ever ask me for anything again."

Guy lay on the top bunk staring at the photo stuck to the ceiling. Standing outside the family home, the familiar dark green Georgian door behind them, his mother, father, brother, sister and two nephews all smiled into the camera. His camera, the photograph was meant to capture their last reunion before he left for sunnier climes again. His father looked relaxed; his shirt sleeves were rolled up, one hand in the pocket of his loose corduroys the other wrapped around a glass tumbler. Mum had her arms around the two grandchildren; the stillness of the picture did not disguise the squirming in their stances. They squirmed, she grinned, good old mum. One day he would make that old bastard proud of him, one day his father would see that, despite not being the most dutiful of his children, Guy could be relied on when really needed.

Guy let a sigh escape, breaking the silence of his small world, Dad would never appreciate how, when everything else had been taken from you, a decent meal and a drop of good nectar could make you feel like the richest man alive.

-3-

Matthew, 1975

"Mrs Isaacs, Matthew is struggling in class. His reading and writing skills are far below average and I'm afraid, at this rate, your son will be leaving school almost illiterate." Mr Parham peered over his spectacles, his thick, bushy grey eyebrows flicked upwards, giving him the look of an eccentric professor.

"Well I don't know what you expect me to do about it. I've tried my best, it hasn't been easy you know. You're the ones what's meant to educate him. He just can't seem to get it, he's not a stupid kid, he loves looking at his books." June Isaacs squashed her palms together and squeezed her hands between her large thighs. God she needed a fag. She felt like a school kid herself sat here in front of this old bastard. She glanced at the wall clock mounted above the blackboard. Her time was nearly up, only another minute or so and he would be keen to wrap this up and move on to the next parent.

"Mrs Isaacs" he looked at the woman in front of him and knew that he was wasting his time. His conscience and a sense of duty kept him going, "if you want your son to gain any qualifications in life, it is my opinion that he would benefit from private tuition. The special needs that your son has cannot be met adequately in the classroom alone. He only has another year left, a lot of hard work is required if he is to achieve anything in his exams."

"You know what fifteen year old boys are like. I can't get him to do anything he doesn't want to. It's not like I've got a husband to back me up. If you ask me, it's these mates at school of his that are the problem. I can't control what he gets up to with them."

Mr Parham glanced surreptitiously at his wristwatch. "When you're ready Mrs Isaacs, I have some very useful contacts I would be happy to share with you. I think Matthew needs to knuckle down, more discipline and some individual help with his studies," he paused for a moment, holding June Isaacs eye. He found it hard to sympathise with this blousy, middle aged woman. Her fuchsia lipstick bled into the smokers lines that radiated from her lips, it distracted him and he constantly found himself watching her mouth. "Well, anyway, thank you for coming today." He stood up, stretching his arm across the pile of exercise books on his desk. June Isaacs bent down and picked her worn out leather handbag off the floor, as she shook his hand she felt the weight of expectation on her. "I'll do my best."

Matt was leaning against his mothers dark green Escort absentmindedly picking at the rubber seal surrounding the rear window. The street was lined with terraced houses, without driveways the cars were parked on the road underneath lime trees which deposited their sticky sap onto the bonnets. The lucky few overlooked the school playing field, a precious patch of green within the crowded rows of housing. Matt watched a small group of children kicking a football around the scorched grass, every now and then one would throw a cautious look his way. His clothes were suspiciously newer and more expensive than most of the other kids. His slim legs were hugged by a pair of Wrangler jeans, his Puma sneakers kept white with constant spit wiping. A bloke appeared on the other side of the playing field. Black jeans, black t-shirt and a Teddy Boy quiff. A small white dog trotted alongside him, one of those Scotty dogs on the end of a thin blue lead, a bit too girly for a bloke. Maybe he was a faggot. Matthew watched him intently. The faggot approached the group of boys and called to one of them, Matt could just make out something about dinner. The shirtless kid grabbed a t-shirt off the bundle of clothes that made for a goal post, he spun it round turning it into a twisted piece of red cotton which he then tied around his waist. The faggot had started walking away again, his skinny back to Matthew. As the kid caught up with him he slung his arm around his shoulders and squeezed him. So he wasn't a faggot; just a Teddy Boy dad walking his wife's pathetic dog.

Peering through his mane of dark hair he spotted his mother walking across the playground towards him. For a moment he toyed with the idea of getting rid of the cigarette he was smoking but no, fuck it, she had no right to lecture him on that subject. As she grew closer he could see the frown, her

33 Dirty Luggage

stride becoming more purposeful as she noticed the white stick in her son's fingers.

"Put that out, get rid of it."

"You're a fine one to talk."

"Yeah, well, I'm your mother. I've just had an ear-bashing in there. You're doing no good Matthew. What do I have to do?" The heat was making June sweat. The nylon dress was clinging uncomfortably to her back, she wanted to lift her arms to the sky and fan her armpits. She resisted the urge, she hated the flapping of the loose skin on her upper arms and had trained herself not to wave them.

"Stop fucking going on." He threw the cigarette on the floor and squashed it with a turn of his foot.

"Come on, get in," she called over the car roof as she unlocked the drivers door.

He looked at his mum, the scowl hardening her features, her mouth puckered into a tight line. She was going to go on at him all the way home, he just knew it.

"Don't reckon I'll come home just yet mum"

"What do you mean?"

"Made plans to meet up with Spider."

"Not that flash Harry. You're gonna get yourself into trouble with the law Matthew. You're coming home, get in the car *now*."

"No, fuck off mum" he turned his back and started walking along the tree lined street towards an alleyway that ran between two rows of terraces.

"*Matthew!*" June watched her son walking away from her, the arrogant swing of his hips, hands in his pockets, shoulders slouched, she just couldn't seem to get through to him anymore. The sigh escaped her lips, a sad, powerless note that hung between the evening calls of the birds in the trees above her.

"Reckon?" Joshua Ryder indicated the house across the road, his hands remained in his pockets, only his eyes moved, sliding in the direction of a well kept detached house. The driveway was empty and on a warm summers evening all visible windows were closed. "Yeah mate, could be a goer."

35 Dirty Luggage

Matt looked up and down the street, a quiet avenue, there was no passing traffic and no one out on their front lawns. There was a respectful space between each house, enough room for driveways, garages and mature trees. The two boys glided across to the house, looking left and right constantly. Without a word passing between them Matt approached the heavy oak front door while Joshua walked across the neat, square lawn to the wooden gate at the side of the house. Hedgerow bordering the lawn offered some concealment if they kept their bodies low. Peering through the small pane of glass Matt pulled the iron ring, a solid, chiming 'ding dong' filled the interior hallway. There was silence. He stepped sideways and looked through the large bay window to the right of the front door. Floral curtains, with matching pelmet, framed the leaded light glass. The room was large, divided by French doors. At the front was the lounge space. A three piece suite, upholstered to match the curtains, was angled around a large television. Several heavily gilded paintings lined the walls and the mantelpiece boasted solid silver photo frames. The French doors were pulled back and Matt could see through to the dining room. A highly polished mahogany table was surrounded by eight queen Anne chairs, a large vase overflowing with long stemmed roses, a handful of petals lying on the glassy surface broke the inanimate appearance of the space. The room ended in patio doors that led to a well manicured back garden. Matt ran a few mental checks, he could see no dogs bed, blankets on the furniture or leads and wellies in the front porch. The back garden seemed to be fenced at a height he knew Spider and he could manage in an emergency. He took all this in as he walked across the front of the house and joined Spider at the side gate.

"All looks okay but it's a dodgy time of day mate" Matt was nervous, the sky glowed warm orange, the grasshopper's chirruping was gaining momentum before the night drew in. Evenings were tricky, you could easily be caught out by people returning home from work.

Spider grinned "It'll be worth it, I know where we can score some good shit tonight." Matt resigned himself to the task ahead of him, taking a deep breath he gave Spider a leg up over the gate. Standing on his own at the front of this strangers house Matt felt the pulse in his neck. Just as he heard Spider pull the bolt on the gate a bicycle turned into the road. It's rider wearing a white short sleeved shirt and a pair of shorts, he had the look of an office worker who changes to ride his bike home at the end of the day. Matt could just make out a briefcase strapped to the back with bungee cords. Middle aged and middle class he looked like a typical resident of the avenue. Matt turned his back, looking under his hair and sideways towards the cyclist. The pulse in his throat was becoming louder, the adrenalin beginning to course through his body. The bike was getting closer, the whirring of the tyres on the hot tarmac becoming audible. Finally the gate swung open and Matt quickly stepped into it, managing to close it just a fraction before the cyclist grew parallel to the house. As that flock of butterflies settled in his stomach they were kicked into flight again as the boys approached the back door. Spider pulled the arm of his sweatshirt over his hand and tried the handle. It didn't budge. Matt scanned the back of the house, an obvious weakness was the small fanlight open in the kitchen. Whispering, they discussed strategy. "Right mate, first thing, lock the side gate again. Then I'll climb on your back to reach through that window, I should be able to reach the latch of the bigger one. Once we're inside make sure the front door is locked, bolted you know?"

Matt nodded. It was the usual kind of plan. Spider, like his nickname, was tall with long limbs. He had the appearance of someone who couldn't keep up with their growth. Inches spurting onto his legs and arms, all bone and sinew, the growth was too rapid for any fat to collect. He was usually the one leaning through, climbing over, unless of course Matt was on his own, which he had tried on two occasions now. Matt bent over, bracing his hands on his knees as Spider clambered onto his back. Grunts of discomfort vibrated in his throat as the soles of Spiders shoes wobbled around on his spine, sweat prickled on his forehead, the air was saturated with a muggy warmth. His nerves were alerted to the sound of young children whooping and laughing a couple of gardens along. Finally, Spider jumped down, a large grin spread across his face, a mischievous twinkle in his eyes "Come on then Paws." Matt returned the grin, now he was Paws, a nickname he had

39 Dirty Luggage

picked up the first time he had broken into a house. Using a knife to slide between the panes of a sash window, he had leant on the glass with a bare hand, his sticky fingered print had left an identifiable calling card. He scraped his belly along the window sill as he pulled himself through the open window, his hands walking along the worksurface and then down the front of the kitchen cupboard. Slithering like a snake, his body stretched out until, curling into a heap on the cold, tiled floor. A moments pause, both standing in the spacious kitchen, internal radars scanning for noise within the house. A clock in the hallway, emitted a single chime. Spider whispered from the corner of his mouth "You take upstairs." Matt nodded in reply.

His footsteps were soft on the deep, plush carpet that lined the hallway. The brown pile was brushed in lines from vacuuming, and Matt couldn't help but flatten the carpet where he trod. The staircase was central, the bottom step opposite the front porch. On one side a wood veneer door led to the lounge, on the other a study, Matt would leave that to Spider. He brushed up the stairs, his heart bouncing like a rubber ball in his chest, salty sweat running from his upper lip into the corners of his mouth. Photographs lined the wall, a family gallery - graduation shots in front of cloudy blue screens, a young couple with a new baby, a studio shot the edges mistily rolled into the gilt frame. Black and white wedding photographs of older generations, the disconnected, stiff subjects probably long since passed. He ran his hand along the wall, the wood chip wallpaper beckoned to be picked, the nail of his middle finger had the satisfaction, sticking it underneath and peeling off the chips like scabs. Posh fuckers could afford to have it fixed anyway. He knocked each photograph, you never knew what might slip out, a trail of wonky photos and ripped wallpaper followed him to the landing. Scanning the bedroom doors he chose the one at the front of the house, the biggest, might hold the jewellery. He pushed the door fully open with his shoulder. He was struck by the floor to ceiling curtains. Huge orange flowers swirled on a brown background, mandarin petals that glowed with the setting sun. For a moment they bedazzled him and he felt unsure that the room was indeed empty. He refocused and scanned. A large wooden box sat centrally on a dressing table at the bay window. Lifting the lid he sifted through handfuls of beads, underneath he discovered a small ring box. Resting on the velvet cushion were three rings. Probably inherited, they were old fashioned in design but each held precious stones, rubies, diamonds, sapphires. Might be worth something, Paws squeezed them into a tight pocket at the front of his jeans. He then pulled out each drawer from the table, three on each side. He had to wiggle them annoyingly to get them out, far easier just to throw them on the floor then try and wiggle them back in. He threw the contents onto the bed, waiting for a heavy thud as something worthwhile fell from the drawer containing her underwear. There it was, a black velvet rectangular case. He chucked the drawer on the floor and pushed the knickers and bras out the way. He held the case, relishing the moment of discovery. It creaked open, a solid gold Albert chain. Must weigh a few ounces. He knelt down and slipped it into his sock, the cool metal against the sensitive skin of his arch made him shiver. He smiled to himself, that was one he was keeping for himself. His eyes fell on the lace and silk underwear lying on the bed. He ran his hand through the coloured satins, his fingers tracing the crutch on a pair of cream knickers. Lifting a bra in front of him he tried to imagine the breast that would fill it. He resisted the urge to take a pair of knickers home, he had to get a move on. He turned his attention to the bedside table, the male side. A small functional clock sat on top of a crime novel. A pair of gold framed spectacles sat cross legged against the bendy lamp. He pulled out the top drawer and tipped the contents on top of the underwear. Amongst the pens, lighters, scraps of paper and aftershaves a gold watch slipped out, a classic Longines, very nice, be worth a few quid. Paws squashed it down into his front pocket. Pulling open the drawstring on a sunglasses pouch, he discovered pair of metal framed Ray Bans. Cool, he sat them on top of his head. He heard the light thud of running up the staircase. He froze in his stance, holding his breath until Spider stuck his face round the door. He was pale, his pupils large with fear, he hissed "The old bill mate. I just spotted one hiding behind the hedge out front" Matt's head spun, "the back." Both boys ran to the back bedroom overlooking the garden. A man in a white shirt and black trousers was climbing over the neighbouring fence.

Wide eyed with terror the boys looked at each other. Spider ran out to the landing, his eyes flicked in every direction, a caged animal looking for it's escape. "The loft, the loft, quick." Matt looked up to the terrifying white square above his head. Already in the grips of adrenalin new surges rushed through his body. "Fuckin' ell Paws, give me a leg up." Numbly Matt responded, he felt his movements in slow motion as he bent down and entwined his fingers. He concentrated on the carpet as Spider's weight balanced on him. He could hear the scraping as the hatch was pulled back. "There's a ladder!." Matt couldn't bear to look as he heard the creaking of the metal and then the crash as Spider unlatched it to the floor. Spider was off him and skimming up the ladder like a monkey. "Come *on* Paws." Matt breathed out, he didn't know what was worse, facing the old bill or the horror of the loft. Spider screamed under his breath "*I am fucking pulling this thing up*" Matt looked up. Anger, panic and frustration were etched into every crease of his friend's face. He took hold of the ladder with each hand and robotically put one foot above the other until he was sat in the dark uncomfortable space of his nightmares. Spider was busy leaning out of the hatch and pulling the incriminating ladder up behind them. He then threw the hatch across and the boys were left with the darkness and the sound of their breathing.

Matt was falling into the whirlpool of another panic attack. His pulse was racing, he was sure his heart would explode, his chest hurt so much. He could not swallow, could not speak, his mouth felt like a desert. The darkness was a double edged sword, on the one hand he was grateful that Spider could not see the blind fear on his face but, on the other, visions were starting to infiltrate the corners of his mind, visions he thought he had forgotten.

Without warning the hatch lifted. Light illuminated the boys faces, a torch blinding them. Squinting they struggled to focus on it's source. From behind the arc of white light a voice spoke.

"Well, look who it isn't. Just can't bloody help yourselves can you. Are you going to jump down or are we gonna have to drag you out?"

-4-

Guy

The grey light of dawn lay on his eyelids like soft white gauze, growing in it's intensity until the light penetrated to the soft egg of the eyeballs beneath. He began to stir, turning away from the embrace of night, like a warm lover that lead him away from his dark reality, allowing him to escape into the colour of his dreams. It had been a strange one that he woke from this morning. He tried to re-capture it, hoping to make sense of the mountain of paper that had been piled on a desk in front of him. There had been an unseen pressure to study it in detail, something made him believe they were his case notes, that awful panic to try and find a hole, a technical hitch in the evidence that would save him from serving this sentence. And there had been blue, the sky or the sea but something that soothed, that tried to stroke the knot in his stomach but it was slipping, something his body didn't lack was sleep and he couldn't force it back onto his mind. Before opening his eyes he listened to the loud calling of a solitary bird who had found a safe spot to land amongst the barbed wire and pigeon proofing that ran along the cell windows. He couldn't identify the species, he had never had much of an interest in birdlife as a child, the quiet and lonely pursuit too boring for his wandering spirit. How he wished he could name that call now, it would connect him to the larger world outside the prison walls, a world where nature existed independently of all the rubbish that men troubled themselves with. He allowed his eyes to lift the shutters and fall upon the photographs on the ceiling, loving, happy faces smiling down at him. He stretched his body the length of the hard single bunk, his pointed toes touching the cold metal bedstead at the end. Another day in paradise, an environment full of empty space, time that needed to be filled, every activity, no matter how small, how inconsequential, planned in detail. Like a hamster tethered to a treadmill, options on or off, how his gut yearned for variety, for the pressure of having too much to do, not enough time to complete it in. At least there was the gym, hours out of his cell walking around the fitness room with a damp cloth. Prison gym's must surely be the cleanest in the world. The jangle of keys outside his door sent a surge of activity through his body as he sat bolt upright, turning to face it. It swung open and a dark haired man stood in the entrance. Possibly a few years younger than Guy the shadows under his eyes and the bristly dark cloud that covered the lower half of his face hinted at a life filled with too many potholes.

"Hi, I'm Guy." He swung his legs over the edge of the bunk.

The deep brown eyes looked up to him, he could see the silent appraisal rolling under the flop of fringe, the usual worries, how mad was he, was he likely to injure him, rob him or drive him crazy with disgusting habits and bad personal hygiene. Guy watched the wide mouth curl into a smile.

"I'm Badger." And he held a large, strong hand up to Guy. It was a firm shake, slightly rough skin, none of that creepy lingering that made you crawl.

"Badger hmm, that sounds like there may a tale attached."

"Yeah, I guess," and the dark eyes shifted downwards briefly.

"Where are my manners, I should get my gear out the way, I'm sure you won't be interested in looking at my rather dry reading material. I'm afraid I've hogged the wall space a bit too, got used to being on my own you see, bit of a luxury being able to spread out in our rabbit hutch of a home."

"I know mate, don't worry I know what it's like."

Guy decided he needed to concentrate very hard if he was to pick up on everything this fella was saying. His voice was soft, his sentences trailing off until the words were barely perceptible. Maybe it was nerves or shyness, hopefully either he would relax or Guy would learn to tune in and this frustrating dialogue wouldn't tire him.

"Do you read much?"

"Not much."

"Oh you'll probably pick it up now you're in here, time on your hands and all that."

"Yeah, probably."

Guy jumped down and moved his pile of books and notepad off the bottom bunk, he was surprised to find Badger was a few inches taller than him. "You're okay with the bottom?"

"You were here first," and he flashed a large grin towards him. It was surprising how much it changed his face. The shadows disappeared behind laughter lines, his brown eyes softened, and he looked younger, cheeky even. He had already started pulling the sheet across the bed, smoothing out the creases and tucking the sides in tightly.

"I've got a cushty number working in the gym" Badger looked up from the mattress. "Really? You're doing alright then."

"Yeah, trying to keep my nose clean," Guy hoped that Badger picked up on the hidden message. He didn't want anything going on in the cell that could jeopardise his progress in the system.

"Don't need to worry about me, I'm gonna be doing the same."

Badger turned his back to him again as he continued to make the bed. Presuming the conversation over Guy decided to get dressed, not that it was a major task. Slipping off the underpants he wore at night for clean ones and then pulling on tracksuit bottoms and his gym orderly t-shirt, job done.

51 Dirty Luggage

Holding the can under his top a puff of deodorant flooded the cell. "You can borrow it if you need to, I know it can take forever to get your order sorted."

A grunt, accompanied by a smile this time "Thanks but they gave me some in my pack."

"I'm going to work in a minute so you'll have a bit of time to yourself. Please take some of my pictures down, just put them on the bed and I'll have a sort out when I get back."

There was a tingle, the flutter of a butterfly's wings as you walked around the prison during 'freeflow'. All doors were opened allowing inmates with jobs or lessons to head to their destinations. Dangerous human beings streamed from the wings, conversations with friends from other areas could take place, drugs slunk from hand to hand, disputes settled, violence erupting, the rapid burst of the siren calling backup for the witnessing officer. Security lined the walls like sentries, faces serious and hard, trying to look colder than the disturbed souls they guarded. Guy felt the tiny nobble of puff like a stone between his buttocks, an uncomfortable but worthwhile compromise to keep the main dealer on his wing happy, he was not a man you wanted to have a problem with, taking pride in creative ways to injure people, Guy did not want to give him any opportunity to practice his art. His job was to pass it to another inmate who was due in the gym later that day. His footsteps were soft and squelching as his trainers rolled along the concrete floor, voices bounced off the stark white walls of the corridor that led him away from the wings and to the prison fitness area. Up ahead he could see a small cluster of men, hands held high, eyes cast to the ground, the stark strip lighting projecting a deathly pallor on their faces like patients in a hospital. Between their bodies he caught glimpses of a security cap. Shit, there must be searches going on. As the small cluster broke away and continued their journeys he saw the liver and white bounce of a spaniel. Bollocks and double bollocks. The clack of the dog's nails on the polished floor grew increasing louder in tune with Guy's heartbeat which threatened to start hitting his chest cavity. Hands in pockets he fixed a gentle smile on his face. Two rough male voices were behind him, he slowed his pace hoping to camouflage himself within their company, but the dog just kept coming tongue hanging out and an expression of pure joy on the flappy eared face. He caught the officers' sharp eye and gave a small nod in acknowledgement. On noticing Guy the dog spotted another game to play, pulling at it's leash to catch a good sniff of this new human. It's nose pressed into Guy's trousers, a soft pushing up and down. With horror he watched the fat little body wiggling, a lovable creature trained to convey messages of doom. He prayed silently that the bottom would stay in the air, the tail wagging as the small dog worked. And then, donk, the dog sat down at his feet, craning his head back to the handler.

"Oh dear" the supercilious smile of the thin lipped officer, had he looked at Guy in that way on the outside he knew he would have been pulverised, "Looks like you're coming for a search."

It had been a close call. Dad's compromised principles had saved him again. The officer in charge of strip searching that day had been in on the tip scam. To the dog handler's consternation, he had conveniently found nothing. His next worry was his cellmate. There was no way that dog loving bastard was accepting that his 'pet' had got it wrong and he would have directed that powerful nose all over his cell. He hoped to god that Badger didn't have anything on him, it would be the worst possible start. His legs felt like concrete as they pounded heavily on the treadmill. The bright red lights that were supposed to imitate a hill run did nothing to motivate him. Even worse, he was surrounded by nonces. It was the vulnerable person's session time in the gym. Paedophiles, rapists and grasses. He kept his head down and tried not to look at the child loving faces that sweated and stroked the machines around him. He would make sure he gave the place a damn good scrub tonight. He was trying not to watch the small group of men on the other side of the room. The free weights were organised in front of a mirror that spanned the length of the wall, the leader of the pack was grunting as he lifted dumb bells, the veins on his biceps purple bubbles under the surface of his black skin. A strange concoction of sexual confusion his eyebrows had been plucked into severe little lines, his hairless arms and legs shining with perspiration. Between sets he would stare at his body in the mirror, twisting and tensing his limbs to survey the definition in his muscles. His 'assistant' moved in affected poses as he bent up and down picking up the used weights. Flirtatious giggles punctuated the clunks and bangs as heavy weights were dropped onto the foam mats. He was far leaner than his 'boss', a nervous metabolism that would struggle to keep weight on. Guy guessed that was part of his popularity, his small frame. Catching the flicker of Guy's stare he blew him a kiss in the mirror. A tight fist in Guy's stomach threatened to force a lump of vomit into his throat. He pressed the speed button down on the treadmill and burst into a loud, thundering sprint as he sent the anger coursing down his legs. A small voice whined beside him.

"Excuse me, excuse me." Guy looked down at the thin, pale little man, his red hair was brushed backwards from his forehead, small unruly curls flicked over his ears. He pressed the pause button on the machine and his legs thudded to a stop.

"Yes?"

"The toilet is blocked, it fills to the bowl every time I try to flush it."

Oh fucking great day this was turning out to be.

Guy stood quietly, listening to the retreating footsteps of the guard that had closed the cell door behind him. The long figure of his new cellmate was stretched the length of the bottom bunk. "Please tell me they didn't search the cell."

"Yeah, they did. There was nothing to find."

With relief Guy sat on the metal chair. "Thank god, I'm sorry about that mate. Dog caught me running an errand for somebody, luckily I've got a bit of a scam on the go and the screw gave me a rain check."

Badger leant up on one elbow, renewed interest sparkled in his eyes. "Must be a good one."

"Yeah, I'll tell you about it someday. Anyway tell me what you've got going on here."

Dirty Luggage

In the centre of the bunk free wall of the cell a large map of the world had been blue tacked.

"It's my plan, I'm planning a new business for when I get out of here." Guy looked sideways at the man lying on the bottom bunk, small feverish spots glowed from the top of his cheeks, he was grinning as he stared at the map. "Oh yeah?"

Badger lay back on the bed, his hands linked behind his head, he spoke to the mattress above him rather than to Guy sitting on the chair.

"Yes. Meat, there is money to be made in meat."

A small finger of unease was tapping itself on Guy's brain "Meat?"

"That's right, I've signed up for a butchery course. This 'ere is my market." Badger extended a pale arm towards the map, his dark hair ran thick along his forearms.

"Well Badger, when I look at that map all I notice are the blue expanses. The oceans are my home " before Guy could finish his sentence Badger had jumped up and was towering over the chair. Guy felt himself lean backwards to avoid the large gestures and occasional spittle from the excited man in front of him.

"Oh me too, me too! Do you dive? I love diving, it's magical, it's like heaven, it feels like you're close to God, do you know what I mean?" he was looking eagerly at Guy who felt forced to come up with a reply that would please the expectant face looking down at him.

"Oh definitely, I have to agree that it certainly is one of the most peaceful experiences to be found on our planet."

"Yes, yes, that's what I mean" and Badger turned back to the map. "This, this place is just about survival. I'm going to do more than just survive Guy, I'm not going to struggle along like the rest of 'em." His hands were on his hips as if delivering a powerful speech to the wall. Guy began to question his first impression of the quiet and broken man that had stepped into the cell this morning. "What are you reading Guy?" The question came quietly and softly, a rapid step down from the exuberance that had just filled the atmosphere.

"Oh uh.." Guy twisted back to the desk, picking up the pile of books, placing them on his lap he turned back to Badger, "well, a little non-fiction, a bit of self education actually, I am also tinkering with a loose plan but one that would force me to stay landlocked." He held up the first two books, one in each hand.

"Oh, wine."

"Yes." He put the two books back onto the small melamine desk. "And then some fiction for escaping." He held the books in the air again for Badger to see.

"Oh, what's that one?" He indicated the large paperback by a well published crime writer.

"It's quite good actually, a bit trashy perhaps but a decent enough read nevertheless. The usual, boy gets badly abused and abandoned by crap parents. Grows into a psychopath with revenge on the brain. Bit of incestuous love and boom, there you have it, a money motivated serial killer."

Badger went very quiet, his eyes absorbing the front cover of the novel. Guy continued holding the book aloft, not quite sure whether to put it down.

"Could I borrow it?"

"Of course, I've finished it, I'm about to start the other one."

Badger grinned as Guy passed him the book. Opening the front cover he curled himself into the bottom bunk.

Guy put his pen down and stretched his arms to the ceiling. The small, caged window above the desk was a dark square, the world outside was black. He twisted round to look at his cellmate. Lying on his side, facing the wall, he was still reading. Guy hadn't heard a peep from him for at least two hours.

"Hey Badger, it's nearly lights out man. How you getting on with the book?"

The bed creaked as Badger slowly rolled over, leaving the book face down on the bed. For several seconds he just stared. His eyes seemed black and his unshaven face seemed to cloak him in shadow, against the white of his forehead it struck Guy that he was indeed looking at a badger. He would not have been surprised if he had opened his mouth to reveal a line of evil little teeth. He couldn't help but wonder why he felt accused of something.

"What's up mate, you don't like it?"

"No, I love it." The gloom lifted as his face broke into a smile, "It's just so sad, it makes me feel angry."

"Oh you mean the way the young boy was treated by his father?"

"Yes, I can understand it."

"Your parents not the worlds best then?"

"You could say that. I just really love this book. Do you mind if the light stays on just another half an hour?"

"Sure, no worries." Guy mused to himself whilst brushing his teeth. This was going to be an interesting relationship.

-5-

Matthew, Mexico 1979

Her skin was so smooth, caramel coloured it smelt of cocoa butter. She was lying on her side, her back towards him, the little ridges of her spine visible. Her long black hair flowed across the white pillow case, glossy like smooth liquorice. He traced the contour of her body, her waist tensed as his fingers tickled this sensitive area. His hand then ran out over the soft curve of her hips, his left hand coming to rest on the top of her thigh. He smiled as she murmured a soft sigh. The late sun was streaming through the open shutters, passing through the mosquito net and onto the two lovers lying naked on the bed. It caught the dust in the air and highlighted the soft down on her body. The air was heavy with the constant assault of motorbikes and old trucks that growled and honked in the street below. Fingers of diesel rose into the warm air and drifted into the open window. He was young and with the virility of a twenty year old, ready to go again. They had at least another hour before her mother returned home from working. The old dog that sniffed and scratched around the

63 Dirty Luggage

courtyard would bark an early warning to them. He ran his hand from the top of her thigh down to the crease where her buttocks met her legs, his fingers straying into the back of her vagina. She still felt wet. Although she had, had enough, she was young and naive enough to want to continue to please him. She rolled over, her breasts tumbling towards him, captivating him with her dark, coffee coloured nipples. He cupped a firm bosom in his hand, bringing his head down to tease the nipple with his teeth.

She looked down at the top of his head, the sun had left fine threads of gold in his dark hair. His broad shoulders were suntanned, his muscles well contoured. The necklace she had made him, wooden beads thread onto leather, hung from his neck, it reached his chest where it swung sexily between his pectoral muscles.

"Matty."

"Yes?" He let the nipple drop from his mouth as he looked up at her.

"You love me?"

"Of course I do."

"Very much?"

He looked into the dark pools of her eyes, her black velvet eyelashes lining them soulfully. "Why?"

"What will happen?" She looked down, a frown on her forehead as she struggled to find the words. "How can be with you, my home is here, yours is England."

He felt his erection softening, he had to turn this around somehow. "Come with me, come to England."

"But how, I Mexican girl, mama and papa will be unhappy you know? Only sixteen, too young."

Matt when quiet for a moment. She was beautiful, the most beautiful girl he had ever slept with. His eyes focused on her full lips, they were so inviting he just wanted to shove his cock in her mouth. Then it came to him. "I know." He looked into her eyes, they were so trusting, so loving. "Let's get married" as he voiced the words a small cloud of doubt floated across his sub-consciousness.

"What?"

She didn't know everything about him, but why should she? He wasn't in England now, it was his past, what he was then wasn't who he was now, why should he have to tell everyone he met that he'd just spent the last few years of his life in and out of prison. It would only get in the way, she might judge him. "Let's get married!"

She giggled "True?"

"Why not? We'll get married and then you can come to England with me, I'll earn some money and we'll travel the world together"

The full lips curled into a smile. "Okay Matty Isaacs, I say yes"

"Good" he pressed his lips down on to hers, forcing his tongue between them. His erection began to press against her thigh. He rolled on top of her, kneeing her legs apart. His cock pushed itself inside the wet warmth of her vagina.

The English churches didn't feel so welcoming as the warm Mexican iglesias of her childhood. British churches were grey and austere, the cold of the climate seeping into the stonework. Nieve forced herself to continue attending Mass, although now, without the presence of round, brown faces, it felt more like punishment than joy. She had also become desperately conscious of the Confessional box; something she'd avoided for many years. The church was quiet today, mid-week, but her loneliness had drawn her through the solid wooden doors and into it's cavernous insides. Occasionally the weak sun would shine through the stained glass windows, a beautiful blue green light transmitting joy into the authoritative space; but then, no sooner had it arced across the pews, a cloud would deaden the glass again. Her knees were beginning to ache on the flat red cushion She sat back onto the pew and placed the cushion onto the brass hook in front of her. She continued to pray; her eyes closed, she could try and organise her thoughts without having to acknowledge any of the pale faced foreigners that wandered around her. The old ladies were filling the vases with fresh flowers, the green scent of lilies and the sweetness of freesias tickled Nieve's nose, fulfilling her vision of England as a green and pleasant land. Soft earth, rolling hills and meadow flowers. The concrete and rain soaked reality had been a terrible disappointment and she wondered how long it would take for the brown to leave her skin and turn her ashen like the sad figures that brushed past her on the crowded High Streets.

A rattle indicated the curtain of the Confessional being opened; it's last occupant leaving it empty, waiting for another troubled soul to fill its' space. She looked over her shoulder towards the ornate wooden cubicle. The Priest was still inside and no-one appeared to be moving towards it. The box's presence pressed at her. She turned towards the altar and crossed herself.

She walked over slowly; if someone entered before her than it was a sign that she needn't seek Penance today. There was no-one around and the Priest was still waiting. She entered the booth, the scent of ancient Oak and wood rot enveloping her, and pulled across the heavy Damask curtain.

"Bless me Father for I have sinned. It has been one year since my last confession." Nieve looked to the silhouette behind the grille. She could just make out his short dark hair and the gleam of a pair of spectacles. He was young enough not to be grey. "I struggle with my choice of husband Father." The first words seemed to crack from her throat. "I er…".

"I'm here to listen." His voice held the reverberation of a large male but it's tone was gentle.

"He's a criminal Father."

"And you knew this when you met him?" There was no change in his pitch.

"A little; yes, I knew. I fell so in love, and I think I his only friend."

"What are his crimes?"

"I not sure Father. He steal things when he was young boy, in houses. Now he promise me, I make him promise."

"But you doubt him?"

"We have money and then nothing. I can see, er…." Nieve struggled to find the word she was looking for. "In his face, not true."

"You can tell he is lying to you."

"Si, yes. But he is my husband Father."

"You need to help him."

"Yes Father."

"Tell me, does he Believe?"

Nieve shifted the weight from her knees to her toes. Her fingertips rested on the smooth wooden ledge of the grille. She focused on collecting the energy from all the other souls that had placed their hands in the same place, imagining the wood transforming into their fingertips placed on hers.

"I show him Father, he has good heart. God will see."

The wooden cubicle resonated with the worldly advice from the young man behind the grille. "We should not abandon those in most need of our help. You must guide your husband to the Church, he must understand his sins and seek forgiveness for them. 'Let him know that whoever brings back a sinner from his wandering will save his soul from death and will cover a multitude of sins.' "

It was raining outside, the wind driving fine needles into the back of Nieve's head and lifting the bottom of her coat. She wanted to run, get home quickly, but she found the cold paralysing, her muscles stiff and unbending. She inched along the pavement, eyes cast to the concrete as the little voice in her head talked voraciously. Digesting all the Priest's words, sucking the full strength of their meaning. There was no penance; as such; more an undertaking to be guided by the Lord. Matthew needed to be saved and she had been given the task.

It was almost a surprise when she found herself standing outside the front door to their block of flats. Her hands were chilled to claws and she struggled to feel the key in her fingers; mind you, the door was so rotten and the lock so loose a hard shove would probably open it. The stairwell echoed with her scuffing footsteps, her cold toes unbending. As she passed her neighbours' doors she caught wafts of their dinners and the faint murmurings from their televisions. She managed to fumble her front door open and was greeted with an empty home; Matty was still out. Still wrapped in her damp coat, she stood at the window that overlooked the children's play area. She could just make out the slim silhouettes of two teenage boys sitting on the swings, the ends of their cigarettes glowing orange in the five o clock darkness. Lighting her own cigarette she sat on the ledge and cracked open the window. The cold air charged sharply into the room, she gripped her coat closed at the neck as she blew the smoke into the space outside. Once the cigarette had burnt down to the faintest slither above the spongy, fibrous tip she rubbed the hot embers against the brick wall outside the window and flicked the butt to the ground two storeys below.

Time to warm the place up again. She closed the window and drew the floor length purple curtains across. The cylindrical lamp in the corner glowed in the same hue as the curtains and the larva lamp threw bulbous, floating shadows across the walls. Taking advantage of Matt's absence she turned the gas heater onto full belt and dropped a rhythmic, sun soaked Samba album on the record player.

Hunger grumbles rolled round in her stomach. She walked over to the kitchenette and, opening the fridge, toyed with the few plastic pots and jars that did a bad job of filling the shelves. Two eggs left, a tortilla for supper. She pulled the heavily used, black frying pan from the shelf that ran over the sink and clunked it on the stove, hanging her damp coat over the rail of the oven. As she was bent over with a match, nervously lighting the gas hob, she heard the jingle of Matt's keys outside the front door.

"Hi honey I'm home!" he laughed as he walked over to her, kissing the back of her neck as she watched over the pan.

"Mmm hmm, you had a good day?" she turned towards him, her mouth set in a grim line

"Oh yeah baby. Look at this." He pulled a wedge of notes from his back pocket, held together with an elastic band.

"How did you get that?"

"Hard work baby, hard work. I had a good day at the auction houses. Sold some lovely old silver and now we can think about our next trip. Where d'you fancy?"

"Matty, I am not sure you are true with me." She looked into his eyes, her eyebrows pulling together in a tight knot

"What do you mean?" He took a step back away from her.

"I worry. I worry that you are doing the things against the law."

"I promised you didn't I? I'm not gonna do anything stupid."

"Yes, you promised me. I say I no marrying a man who goes to prison, and we marry and now you must be true. What is in the bag?"

"What bag?" He pulled his face down into the most serious mask he could pull off.

"I saw it, you put something in the cupboard before you kiss me."

"Oh that bag. That's some stuff I bought in the auction. I'm selling it tomorrow. I tell you babe, we'll be on a plane again before you know it."

"Hmm, I hope you true to me Matty Isaacs," and she turned back to the hob.

He sank into the second hand couch, his backside stretching the South American throw tight across the back of the sofa. He swung both legs up and over the arm. God, she was becoming a pain, he was finding it hard to keep anything from her. He watched her moving around the little kitchen, she was still lovely, far better than anything he had seen around here. And she was his. That was the good thing about marriage, she was his now, even before that he owned her, he was the first man she had slept with. Nothing would ever change that. Things would be better when they got away from here. He had plans.

She handed him a plate and fork before nudging his legs down with her bum and sitting cross legged on the sofa beside him.

"Things will get better won't they Matty."

"Course," he put his plate on the floor. "Come here" he pulled her onto his lap, he meant to talk to her but the firm arse resting on top of his cock began to distract him. "I'm working hard for us baby."

Six o clock in the morning and they were curled up together in bed. Nieve slept with her mouth under the blankets, gaining a little extra warmth from her breath. They didn't usually wake until around eight but something had pricked her consciousness and her eyes opened to the grey morning light. A loud crash came from the living room.

"Police, police, nobody move."

A small cry escaped her lips and she clung onto Matt's back, her nails digging into his sides. He rolled over and looked at her, they were both silent but they stared at each other, her eyes wide with fear, his wide in apology. The door to the bedroom swung open and a police officer stood at the doorway, behind him Nieve and Matt could make out at least two others in the lounge.

"Goodmorning" the officer gave a wide grin at the two sets of eyes peering over the blanket.

'Matthew Isaacs?" Matt nodded. Nieve continued to stare in fear at the officer.

"Have you got any clothes on Miss?"

"Yes." it had been so cold last night she had crawled into bed wearing one of Matts sweatshirts.

"Okay, then I'll ask you both to step out of the bed and join me in the other room."

Nieve and Matt sat shivering on the sofa as the officers turned their little studio upside down. Matt was beginning to feel the anger burn inside. Nieve had stopped looking at him and he knew, at any moment, the police were going to find the jewellery he had come home with last night. He stared at his feet, clenching and unclenching his toes. He knotted his hands together, trying to resist the urge to smash something.

"Okay Mr Isaacs, you're nicked for burglary." Matt looked at the officer, smug faced bastard smiling at him, he would love to shove his fist right into the centre of his old face. He turned to say something to Nieve. She wouldn't look at him. Fuck this, he wasn't having it, he wasn't going to prison again. He went to stand up, as he straightened his legs he shoved his head into the copper's soft stomach. The officer stumbled backwards and wheezily called out for help. Matt grabbed his opportunity and ran for the front door. Two large hands gripped his ankles, sending him tumbling forwards, his chin smashed on the wooden floor, his bottom teeth cutting into his top lip. He thrashed his legs backwards but could not loosen the officer's grip. And then someone sat on him, the heavy weight pushed the air out of his chest, his ribcage digging into the hard floor. A rush of adrenalin burned through his limbs, the rage was like fire through his veins. The anger could not find a physical outlet, he was pinned, face down on the floor. He roared as his arms were yanked backwards.

"Shut up you stupid bastard." The handcuffs were slammed on, adrenalin masked the pain as the metal dug into his wrists.

Nieve watched them bundle Matt out the front door. As the hollers echoed further down the stairwell she stood up and crossed the floor. Closing the front door she leant her back on it as she surveyed the tipped out contents of her home, tears tumbled down her face.

The blue metal door swung open and a prison officer stepped into the small space, he cuffed Matt's shoulder. "You got a new cellmate Isaacs." Matt threw his book onto the bed and swung his legs to the floor. A small, dark Asian man stood smiling at the doorway. His dark eyes glinted over a flat nose, his angular cheekbones drew downwards to a pointy chin. The impression was ferret like. Matt didn't bother standing up, he had been enjoying the silent gloom of his own thoughts and resented this intrusion.

"I'll leave you two gentlemen to it." The screw closed the door and with a jangling turn of the lock, whistled away along the landing.

"You are unhappy I see." The small man threw his bag onto the top bunk. "You cannot keep this place to yourself you know, better you share with me and not some dirty sex pest."

Matt looked at the chatty little man as he started to place his belongings on the small cupboard beside the bunk. He was older than him, probably in his thirties, his lean frame looked sinewy.

"Where are you from?"

"Thailand my friend, and you I think is England yes?"

"Yeah."

"Well, maybe when you feeling happier we can talk but now I am tired and need afternoon rest okay?"

"Sure."

Matt pulled his legs back onto his bunk and picked up his book. He had to turn back a page, the interruption had lost his train of thought. He worked his way over the words, meaning slowly coming to the sentences in front of him.

The buzzer for dinner and Matt knew he would have to wake the little man up. Either that or one of the screws would come in and poke him awake with a truncheon. He stood up and looked at the sleeping face of his new comrade. His closed eyes tilted slightly at the corners and his mouth held the faintest trace of a smile. The impression was of someone completely at peace.

"Ah mate. Mate, you gotta wake up. Time to get some scoff."

The deep brown eyes opened and stared straight up at the ceiling.

"Ah, we have dinner. Some fine british cuisine eh?"

Matt smiled, "yeah mate."

They walked along the landing together to the dinner hatch and took their place in the line of dishevelled and disgruntled fellow inmates.

"Now maybe we can introduce one another. My name is Thammaraja. I come from Thailand but I find that the drug business is more lucrative here instead. I have a few years to spend in this place."

"I'm Matt. Burglary, three years."

Tham formed his words around mouthfuls of processed mashed potato, granular gravy and slippery cabbage. "You work to travel then my friend?"

"Yes."

"And I travel to work. It is funny isn't it. There could be something to learn from this Matt."

Matt eyes Tham's face cautiously. "I have a wife, she doesn't like any of this. She's threatened to leave me before."

"And this wife means a lot to you?"

"Yes, she's a goddess and she's mine. I have to keep her."

"Well, maybe when you living a grand life she'll be happy eh Matt?" Tham laughed, his teeth gleaming white against his brown skin. "For the moment, we eat this shit."

Matt laughed, the little fizz of new horizons, the excitement of wanderlust turning the corners of his mouth into a smile again.

A Friday afternoon. The rain had poured outside their small world all day and it's greying effect was beginning to sink into both men's souls.

"I have been saving something for a day such as this. A friend has sent me a birthday card Matt."

"I didn't know it was your birthday?"

"Ah, not today, but soon. Would you like to share it with me?"

They had been on twenty four hour lock up. Staff shortages meant they were stuck in the cell constantly. It was also the weekend which meant there was no chance of the situation changing either. Matt's head was aching from reading. His eyes were sore and the offer of escaping it all with an LSD trip was tempting.

"Oh, one of those birthday cards!"

"Yes, I have a good friend eh"

"Mmmm, hang on, I've got a new letter from Nieve." He pulled out a sheet of pale blue paper from an envelope that had been sellotaped back together; the prison officers had read it first. Her handwriting looped and slanted in over-exaggerated arks.

"Well, take this little corner and have a read while you wait for our journey to begin." Tham tore a small square off the LSD soaked card and passed it down to Matt who threw it to the back of his tongue and took a dry gulp, forcing the little piece of paper down his throat. "I need a drink!" He stood up and walked over to the jug of water, swishing out the plastic beaker before filling it and taking a huge swig. "Need some?"

"Yes please." Tham put a square of paper on his tongue and gulped the rest of the water down. "Now read your love letter, it will place you in good mind for the trip eh Matty?"

Matt sat on the edge of his hard bed and picked up Nieve's letter. Slowly, he concentrated on her sloping hand.

17th May 1982

Dear Matty

This is difficult letter for me. I sorry if it make no sense but I try hardest. I always say don't be in prison Matty, I don't want husband in prison. It not life I want. I know you do bad things before but you promise me, you say true, no more. But you lie. You lie and it gives me pain. I very unhappy, I try to stay good wife but for too long Matty. I wait for you but I am poor and it no good. I going to have a baby, I no tell you as I no worry you but I cannot have baby on my own. I need a divorce Matty and I can find new husband take care of me. I have seen lawyer and he will write to you.

I sorry Matty but you promise and you lie.

Te ame

Nieve

Matt's anger turned white. The fucking bitch, she couldn't do this. He stared at the metal coils of the bunk above him.

They began to move, slithering along the mattress, raising their heads at him. "Oh fuck."

"Hey, what is the matter my friend?"

"She's divorcing me."

Tham looked at the ceiling, he needed to turn this around,, quickly otherwise they were in for a rough ride. Bad trips in prison ended in straitjackets down the hospital block. He jumped off his bunk and looked at his mate lying stiff as a corpse on the bed. "Give me that letter." Matt handed the evil document to him. "I show you what we think of this stinking letter." Matt watched with interest as Tham untied the waistband of his grey tracksuit pants and pulled them and his underpants to the floor. He grinned at Matt, the devil's twinkle in his eyes. Picking up a lighter he bent over and held it next to his arse, with his other hand he held Nieve's letter behind the lighter. He screwed his face up, the strain creating a crimson glow beneath the suntanned skin until a long squeaky fart squeezed out of his arsehole. He flicked the lighter and a shot of flame caught the letter. He waved the burning letter in front of his face.

"I fart on mindfuck letters my friend. I fart on the people that write them!"

Matt felt his stomach tremble until it clenched in the middle and he was bent double with giggles. "Oh you fucker." He managed to catch his breath and looked at his small, brown friend. "You have the whitest teeth I have ever seen"

"Oh yes, with these teeth I can hypnotise the ladies and the customs people." Tham took a little bow and then walked up and down the tiny cell, three paces up, three paces back. "Look at me, I am a snake charmer." He picked up a black dirty sock lying on the floor. He held it with both hands in a pretend wrestle towards his face. "See how she wants to bite me, see those fangs. Filled with poison eh Matt?"

Matt watched the sock as it swiped and hissed at Tham, he could see the fangs ready to strike, the tiny beaded eyes fixed on it's prey. "Woah mate, that's freaking me out."

Tham laughed. "There is no need to fear, watch." He lay the sock on the floor and created a bridge with his thumb and forefinger. "See how she cannot strike, she is paralysed by my hold. It is the same with the ladies. I hold their throats while I fuck them." Tham began to thrust his pelvis backwards and forwards grunting in time with each thrust forward. "How they love me Matt, especially the dumb white girls. They buy the ganja from me, maybe something stronger, and then they look at me. They believe I am mystical, a brown foreign specimen, I will know sex secrets. They open their wobbly white thighs for me and I show them the serpent" he laughed again, his mouth wide open, to Matt's distorted brain it looked like a cavern. His eyes meandered to the wall behind Tham. The small bricks seemed to be moving in a circular pattern. He slid off his bunk and crawled on all fours to the wall, placing his hands on the cold brick he felt them move, following the bricks down and round. "They are moving, they are showing me they live too."

"Oh yes Matt, everything has life. It is my belief. Look at this table, the wood came from a tree. The tree was alive, it carried life, birdsong, insects. It heard human voices, it felt human touch. It gave birth, it's seed carried for long distances. Just because we have turned it into a table does not mean it is dead no? It still has a memory in it's grain." Matt crawled to the table, resting his cheek on the smooth side. "It comes from the world outside Tham. I want to be out again."

"You will good friend and I will help you. You are young boy, not too stupid I thinking. You like travel and I know people who need travellers. I will give you a contact when you leave here. You carry the old horse for him and you will make good money."

"Oh I don't know. It could be bad karma man."

"No! You give people want they want, what they crave. Everyone has one life, let them choose how to live. This earth gave us opium in her flowers, a little numbness when times are hard."

Matt lay on his back, the cool concrete floor connected him to the cell again. "I could make good money?"

"You will live like a king, or maybe a knight and then you can go rescue your divorcing goddess hmm?"

"That would be really cool Tham." Matt closed his eyes, the smell of cocoa butter lingered in his mind. "Let's dig a tunnel man, we could do it, people always used to."

Matt rolled onto his belly, studying the tiny cracks and fissures in the concrete floor. Tham joined him, their heads together in the small space. "I see ants only Matt, no holes or tunnels. I think there must be another way for you to escape."

"Smoke, oh fuck man we need to smoke."

Matt stood up and opened the top drawer of the table. He found his packet of backy and some papers. Sitting on the edge of the bed he tried to roll a fag. His fingers seemed to get fatter and fatter until he could not even feel the small rolled cigarette between them. He started to giggle. "Look, it's disappearing under these fat sausages of mine, you gotta help me man."

And so they spent the next six hours smoking and talking shit until, finally, their acid riddled minds curled up and died. They both fell into a dream filled sleep, Tham on the bottom bunk, Matt on the concrete floor.

-6-

Guy

Guy walked in the cell to find Badger sitting on his bunk forking tuna straight from the small, circular tin.

"Wow, tuna mate, why the celebration?"

Badger looked up, his eyes were light brown today, his cheeks creased trying to fit in the smile that spread across his face.

"I'm starting my butchers course."

"That's great news, maybe I'll open my tuna as well." Guy felt genuine warmth in his gut as both men laughed in unison.

"Oh yeah mate, this is the start of it. I'm gonna do well at this, I just know it." Badger had begun to focus on the map again as he spoke. "It's going to open a whole new world to me."

Guy followed Badger's gaze, he still didn't get it but then he had no knowledge of the meat trade so he continued to make polite but ignorant noises whenever Badger talked about his business.

"So are you going to come back stinking of blood and guts every night?" Guy smiled down to the fishy smelling man.

"What?" Badger's eye's narrowed and his fork moved down from his mouth.

"I'm only joking mate." Guy found himself wanting to take a mental step backwards from the intensity of Badger's eyes.

"Oh," and his face softened again. "Did I tell you about the id's I came in with?"

"No." Guy scraped the chair around to face him, "Go on."

"Well, when I came in here they found some other id's on me. They're busy trying to trace the owners."

"What kind of id's mate?" Guy wasn't so sure he totally agreed with out and out theft.

"Oh you know, the usual, drivers licenses, credit cards."

"I guess you're worried they'll stick you on for those charges too then huh?"

"No. Not really, there's a couple of German ones and another one from France. They can't trace the owners so I'm alright"

Guy looked up at the map again. "So you've always travelled then?"

"Yeah, since I was a kid, with my dad."

"What did he do?"

"Oh, he was on the road a lot."

"That must have been fun, out and about with your old man."

"Kind of," and Badger rolled over to face the wall, the wide expanse of his back facing Guy. Guy supposed that was that subject closed then.

"Hey, how about you join me for the Mencap day? I need another volunteer."

"Oh, I'm not sure."

"Yeah, you'll be alright, you're strong and I could really do with the help." Badger turned over. Guy knew he would say yes, there was just something ever so slightly sycophantic about their relationship.

Guy loved the Mencap days. Residents of one of the local homes would come to the prison for fitness sessions, basketball, football, ping pong or maybe a go round the gym. A whole range of needs had to be catered for from the mentally retarded to the chronically handicapped, the kind of adults that suffered stares in the street. For Guy it was a day of simplicity, of watching unaffected joy on the faces of people who expected so little in life. But he struggled to find volunteers who felt the same way as him. Many of the inmates felt intimidated or uncomfortable or something. He found it contained moments of beauty in his otherwise ugly environment, taking him away from his own troubles and focusing on the basics, the small, sometimes unusual things that could bring about moments of great tenderness or happiness.

The indoor sports courts were full of squeaky trainer sounds and stale sweat odours. Guy moved swiftly from the equipment cupboard to the different stations, placing basketballs, volleyballs and soccer balls at safe distances from one another. Badger hovered around him, fidgeting with the tension of the nets or the positions of the goals, his nervousness manifested itself in twitchy fingers and thumbs. Guy smiled to himself, all the volunteers suffered the same jitters first time round.

"Okay mate, we're all done in here, let's set up the gym."

They cleared space in the free-weights section, just leaving the lighter loads arranged in a small circuit. "Do you want to be in charge of this area or out on the courts with me?"

"I'll er, I'll work with you if that's alright."

"Sure"

They began notching up basketball hoops until the swish of the double doors signalled the arrival of their charges for the day. Badger held the ball under one arm and stood just one pace behind Guy as they approached the small huddle of extraordinary looking people. Ranging from wheelchair bound, physically disabled to strong looking mentally challenged, all heights, weights and ages huddled in a group of around fifteen. On closer inspection at least four of them were women. All dressed in similar old fashioned and badly fitting clothes they lost all traces of the obvious femininity that other women relied on to make themselves attractive and different from their male counterparts. Amongst the shocking haircuts and wild facial hair they were distinguishable only by their fuller bodies and shorter height. Leading the group was a tall, thin dark haired man, a brush of sparse black hair lined his upper lip and a bristly line of eyebrow hair met across the top of his nose. He stretched out his right arm to handshake with Guy. The movement was slightly twisted as if his arm left his shoulder socket in a corkscrew effect. Guy took the long fingered hand in his, the wrist bones prominent as he pumped his arm up and down.

"Hello Chief, is it a good day?" Guy's posture was slightly deferential before the awkwardly contorted proud man.

"Good day yes Captain." As their hands unclasped the group jostled slightly as a round, firm little man shouldered his way to the front. His smile revealed prominent front teeth with a large gap running between them, giving the impression that they had a life of their own and were pulling away from one anther. His eyes struggled to focus on the space in front of him and tended to roll upwards to the ceiling.

"Ah, Not So Bad, how are you my friend?"

"Not so bad, not so bad." As he reached Guy he raised his right arm, bent sharply at the elbow. Guy raised his left and gripped the strong little man's hand in an over fingered clasp. To the delight of the group, an arm wrestle began and after putting up a good struggle, Guy eventually let his arm tip over. The crowd roared and clapped, several jumping up and down. "Aw, you got me again."

The little man grinned, "You are not as strong as me. You never as strong as me." And he slapped his hands against his chest.

Unnoticed amidst all the noise and excitement a plump girl, her face round with Down's syndrome, had approached Badger. She tugged on the sleeve of his grey t-shirt.

"Are you joining my team?" Badger's eyes were round as saucers as he looked down at the blue eyed face beaming up at him.

"I er, um maybe."

Guy laughed "You better watch her mate, that's Daisy and she is quite a one for the tall, dark and handsome. Okay ladies and gentlemen, it is now time to choose your teams."

Chief turned to face the group, waving his long arms above their heads he began to identify people and indicate they should move from one side to the other. The response was a mix from wide eyed concentration to complete and utter ignorance of the task before them. A couple of younger men, neither of which looked more than nineteen, started to shove one another in the chest.

"Chief, we appear to have a problem." Guy walked into the middle of the group where the two men were now falling backwards with each received shove. Guy gently held the elbow of one and talked quietly into his ear.

"Hey, Johnny, this way mate, I need your help today, you can be my assistant." A lopsided smile slid across up Johnny's face as he allowed himself to be led out to the front and stood next to Badger. His head never looked up from his feet and Badger found himself shuffling his feet imperceptibly away to avoid the bumping of his constantly rocking new assistant.

"Okay, now let's all work this out like friends." Debate and negotiation starting humming between the more sociable members until, in the end, they were in the same groups they were always in. Badger leaned into Guy, speaking from the side of his mouth "Is it always like this?"

"Yep, but for some of them, this is the best bit."

Guy designated Badger to wheelchair patrol, trying to involve and assist anyone with wheels to play. Bending at the waist to propel the wheelchair around the court, the soft jersey tracksuit bottoms pulled tighter across his arse. It proved too much for Daisy who followed him around like a puppy, flashing a blue eyed smile at him every time he turned around. Occasionally she would bounce in front of him, pushing up the little blonde curls that bobbed under her ears. By the end of the first game Guy was bent over in laughter. "Oh mate, that is the funniest thing." Badger's cheeks were red with embarrassment and suppressed anger. He spoke through gritted teeth, "tell her to leave me alone mate."

"Oh no, this is the most fun I've had in ages." As Guy went to turn from him he noticed a sudden flash of cold on

Badger's face, as if someone had quickly tried a monsters mask on, the meanness in his eyes turning them almost glittering black, his mouth a nasty tight line. As he looked again it had disappeared and he was back to the same uncomfortable looking man trying to dodge the attention of the eager-to-please young woman. The bent over man in the wheelchair was oblivious to Badger's feelings, his priority to keep him running. Enjoying the breeze created and the whirl in his stomach as they cornered and raced for the ball, he would open his mouth in a large dark circle and holler until they moved again. If Badger didn't respond immediately he would bang his thick soled lace up boots against the footrests of his chair. As the game had stopped for a breather he was now kicking up a storm, his legs bashing painfully into metal. His hollering was now reaching fever pitch and was beginning to tip over into a scream. Guy took hold of the black handles and began to sing softly, almost in the tones of a lullaby. As he sang he swung the wheelchair gently side to side as he walked around the edge of the hall. The legs stopped and the screaming reduced to a gentle whimper after around thirty seconds. The wasted limbs slowly curled in again and his head dropped further to his chest as the muscles in his neck eased.

Badger had tried to protect himself with movement, joining the volleyball game, but Daisy still managed to place herself within his sight. Joining the opposing team she stood by the net, jumping up and down and calling "Yoo hoo!"

As the day ended Guy was disappointed to see the relief on his cellmate's face.

"Not your bag eh?"

"It was okay." But his voice and face were deadpan.

"Just help me to clear up and then we'll be finished."

They walked around the sports hall collecting the equipment in silence. Guy couldn't help but feel pissed off with the surly looking bloke beside him, he felt his favourite day had been slightly tarnished by the lack of joy on his friends face.

"Oh well, back to your course next week hmm?"

"Yeah." And the gentle smile sat on his face again.

Watching Badger returning to the cell every day Guy concluded that learning suited him. Every night he was full of conversation, most of which Guy tried to tune out to. All the talk of bones, cuts and fat and he started looking at the grey pieces of meat on his tray in a new light. It was not that he wanted to turn vegetarian it was just that he liked some distance between the animal and the wedge of food. It didn't seem to bother Badger though. He had brought him in on the Boeuf Bourguignon evenings but it was starting to lose it's special place in his heart, as he ate Badger would happily talk about which part of the cow this bit came from whilst forking it down his throat. And the descriptions of the knives man, how sharp they had to be to get into this place or do that job, the pleasure it gave him to see how he managed to sharpen it so the meat sliced like butter.

The map had begun to take on a new life too. With everyday of his course under his belt Badger began to plot little routes. He would butcher here and export to there. He was so convincing that, in the end, Guy found himself believing that this bloke really would make his fortune trading meat around the world.

-7-

Matthew

Fucking hell he had to get out. Nieve, Nieve. She was haunting his dreams, his nerves twitched with her every moment he was awake. If Tham wasn't distracting him then he was lost. A dark shadow was growing over his mind. What about the baby? *His* baby. He couldn't let another man have it. And she was his. He knew she loved him still, anyone else would just be a distraction. He had to make her see, he was the only one for her. His heart was trapped in a cage too small, metal bars dug into it, hurting, aching. And these four fucking walls. Immovable, solid. He couldn't do anything. He *had* to get out.

Tham watched Matt as he paced backwards and forwards, his eyes focused on a point on the wall one way and then the other. He hadn't heard a word from his friend for at least an hour.

"Hey Matt, did I ever tell you about the two Americans?"

Matt stopped and looked at Tham quizzically. "Huh?"

"The two Americans, the pot heads, did I tell you the story?"

"No, no I don't think you did." Turning his back to the wall he continued pacing.

"Hey Matt, Matty boy. Let me tell you the story." Tham jumped off the top bunk forcing Matt to stop. "Sit down, sit down." Tham indicated the lower bunk.

"I can't mate, I've got to get out of here."

"Well, unless you have a bomb and a big machine gun, I think you stuck with me again. What is the problem my friend?"

"It's her Tham. I can't get her out of my head. I've got to speak to her."

"Aah, the wife. You know, I have a lot of learning to do in my life but some things I know. I know that these women are trouble. They are good for the sexes yes, a lot of fun, but while they smiling at you, oh yes, oh yeah baby, they are secretly injecting you with their poison. It is a madness of the brain and I very afraid that you have the madness my friend."

"I just need to get out Tham, then I can sort it out. It will all be okay."

"You not have very long left no?"

"Less than a year now."

"Well, maybe you can get home visit. Just a day or two. Go talk to wife, make sense and then come back. Make it all ready for when you finish."

Matt grabbed Tham's shoulders, bringing his eyes level with the dark man's face. So close that Tham reeled from the empty stomached breath and stale sweat that puffed across from his crazy friend.

"You are right. You are right! That is just what I'm going to do. I'll speak to probation, say I'm going to see mum, get everything sorted for when I get out. They'll go for it, they always do. I'll go to Nieve Tham, I'll make her see."

The train slowed as it approached the station, the green fields changing to industrial sized car lots and warehouses. Graffiti scoured the billboards and railway tunnels. Matt grabbed his backpack from the overhead shelf and slung it over one shoulder. Standing by the carriage door he relished the fresh air that whipped across his face through the open window. Before the train halted, with an arm out the window he opened the door, stepping onto the platform just as the train rolled to a stop. The station was loud, buzzing, a central junction with numerous lines converging. Matt struggled to focus on the platform information, reading the signs whilst trying to listen to the nasal announcements over the tannoy system. The sound of his mother's home town bounced at him from the opposite platform, he ignored it and went to scour one of the timetables. Running his finger slowly along the line of Nieve's destination he felt the nips of anxiety increasing as the thought of seeing her face grew closer to reality. He had half an hour to wait before the next train. He was too distracted to kill time with a coffee or a newspaper and preferred to sit on the platform watching the endless movement of people and trains. No-one bothered to sit on the same seat as him, he guessed he looked pretty rough, you kinda lost touch when you hadn't been in the real world for a couple of years. Finally the train screeched into the platform, the squealing from the brakes a welcome sound to the impatient Matt.

After passing several satellite stations covered in grey looking people, Nieve's stop came into Matt's line of vision. A mid-sized southern town, the station consisted of only four platforms. It was calmer and Matt was grateful for the extra head space as he tried to gather his thoughts. He was picturing her opening the front door, baby on her hip. She would smile and then break down in tears. She would beg him not to leave her, tell him how sorry she was. He smiled to himself, yes, he would get her back.

He checked the money in his wallet, just enough to get a taxi he reckoned. He'd keep an eye on the meter.

The taxi turned into a small cul de sac, around ten semi detached houses circled the little close. The front gardens were green with flower borders and hedgerows, the cars mid range, new or just a few years old. How could she afford to live here? He asked the driver to pull over, he wanted to take his time approaching the house. Hands in pockets he walked slowly, a man was mowing the front lawn of a house in the corner. He knew he was being watched, each time the man turned at the end of a line his eyes would slide sideways, trying to weigh up the intent of the stranger walking along the close. It was only the second house along, number three. A blue wooden door around a rectangular bevelled glass window. No car on the drive, no windows open. Matt walked up the flagstone pathway, the grout fresh between the dull pink and yellow pavers. A white milk bottle cage sat next to the front door, a dial indicating one pint daily. He pressed the front door bell, a white button set in a black casing, the ding dong resounding in the hallway. No movement. He pressed it again, and again, and again. He stepped sideways to the front window, cupping his hands against the glass to see through the reflection. The fine weave of the net curtain allowed him to see into the lounge. A deep red velvet sofa lined one wall, on the opposite a television sat on a black ash sideboard, a collection of VHS videos lined up like a bookcase. And there it was, on the wall opposite him, staring him in the face, a Mexican wall hanging. It's bright ribbons and braids, reds, yellows, blues and oranges, twisted and knotted over a piece of dark wood. Pottery faces, round like the sun and moon, jeered and lamented him. It was her. This was Nieve's house.

He turned around, the mower had gone quiet and there was no sign of it's owner. He walked briskly round to the side gate. The top was lined with a strip of metal spikes and a twist of the ring latch confirmed Matt's fear, the gate was locked. He had to go over. A quick rummage in his backpack and he found a jumper, he threw it over the top of the little spikes, they were pretty dull and more a discomfort than a real deterrent. He threw his pack over the gate, no going back now. He gripped the top of the fence and placed a foot midway up the gate. With his leg muscles he pushed himself up, the nasty little spikes wedged into his stomach before he lifted himself again and landed on the crazy paving beneath him. The back garden was small, an oblong lawn edged by a path one side and a flower border the other. He pressed his nose against the kitchen window. A glass dining table, two chairs and a baby's high chair was pushed against the back wall. A few objects had been left on the draining board underneath the window, a child's beaker amongst them. Matt turned back to the garden. The path led to a small shed. Worth a look, never know what you might find, maybe even a spare key. Halfway along the path clothes fluttered on a rotary washing line. Something gnawed at him. He stopped and focused on the washing. Several large white shirts rippled in the breeze. Men's shirts. Matt stepped closer, slowly turning the line, amidst the cotton knickers and tea towels were male underpants and towelling sport's socks. He felt the roar begin to stir in the pit of his stomach.

"*That fucking bitch!*" he ripped the shirts from the line, stamping them into the earth. He pulled socks off, pegs pinging upwards, throwing them across the garden, they landed in the flower beds, on the shed roof. He looked to the line, just the female items remained. He picked up his pack and opened the shed door. The air was close, warm creosote and dust. Dirty garden tools hung on hooks along the back, shelves of paint pots, white spirit, glass jars with stiff paintbrushes. He sat on an upturned bucket, his eyes could just reach the dirty side window allowing him a partial view of the house.

He must have drifted off, his cheek resting against the scratchy surface of the shed, a line of dribble ran from the corner of his mouth. Voices, he could hear something. He straightened his back and peered through the window. There she was, in the garden, a little girl toddling around her feet.

"Que ha sucedido?"

She was bent over, walking around the garden picking up the dirty shirts, collecting them under her other arm. Her dark hair was loose, it tumbled over her shoulders each time she bent over, he could only catch glimpses of her face. She looked thinner, her cheek bones more prominent. He could hear her lilting Spanish as she muttered and cursed to herself. He slowly pushed the shed door open. She heard the creak and snapped her head round to the noise. Her hands flew to her mouth, the washing dropping onto the grass again.

"Matty, Matty, what are you doing?"

"I came to see you Nieve. I wanted to talk to you."

"What are you doing?"

He ignored her question "Who is he?"

"It doesn't matter."

"Is he better than me? Do you love him?"

"Please Matty, please you must go"

"I love you Nieve, you're mine."

"You can't come here. You should not be here. He is a police officer."

"Why? Why have you done this to us?"

"You weren't here, I have a little girl."

"I will make things better for us. You don't belong with him." He looked down at the small child, her pudgy legs wobbled as she leant into the flower bed, hands flapping trying to reach the head of a chrysanthemum. "Is she mine?"

"You cannot be a father. You must go, he will be home any minute."

He stepped towards her, squeezing her cheeks with the fingers of his right hand. "I will come back."

Hitching his pack onto his shoulder he walked out of the side gate. Nieve felt her legs weaken and sank to the grass on her bottom. She called her daughter, laying on her back she let the child clamber over her, kissing and giggling, she tried to lighten her heart.

He stood in the phone box enjoying the warmth as the sun shone through the small panes of glass. A fine layer of cigarette ash coated the handset and dial, little piles collected in the nooks and crannies. He wouldn't be beaten by him, whoever the dirty police bastard was; he was better than all of them, he was going places. One day they'd all regret taking him for an idiot.

He pulled out the crumpled piece of paper from his jeans pocket and smoothed it out on the phonebook shelf. Tham's curly writing made him smile. Fishing around in his pockets he gathered a handful of change. He picked up the receiver and dialled the numbers on the square of paper.

"Hello?"

"Yeah, hi. I'm a friend of the Thai, He thought there was a chance of some work with you."

He loved Bangkok. In a large city, he stood out. He was taller than most and, being a Westerner, he found the girls couldn't leave him alone. At night the Pattaya streets were animated by bright lights, music belched from the strip clubs in competition with the high pitched engines of hundreds of mopeds. Aromatic Asian spices filled the air as food stalls sizzled with meat, enticing hungry travellers and working locals. Matt walked along the centre of the boulevard, like a shark swimming against the tide of pretty Thai women that would throw him sideways glances, their smiles an invitation to purchase their bodies for an hour or two. It was cheaper to keep one for a few days but he found they became too demanding. Easier to fuck them and move on to a different one next time. He took a last drag of the high tar cigarette, so close to the butt that it burnt his throat. He flicked it on the ground and noticed the high heeled white sandals it landed next to. They stopped and the toes pointed in his direction. He followed the slim brown legs up to where they met a white PVC mini-skirt, a bare midriff, the lack of hips almost childlike. A white bikini top concealed an almost flat chest, long straight brown hair hung across the small shoulders. Above the wide smile the brown eyes stared directly at him, a proposition. He smiled back but shook his head. Not tonight. He was on a mission. He was finally meeting Mr Big. After proving himself a reliable and trustworthy mule the guy in charge wanted to meet him. That could only mean good things, more responsibility, more money. He continued walking, eyeing the entrances to the different clubs. Girls leaned provocatively on the doorways, neon signs shining pink and purple on their glossy, sleek hair. The meet was in one of the firm's clubs. A large one, established. Boasting the best girls performing on several stages simultaneously.

At the entrance, a small, hard looking man stood amongst the hip jutting women. Matt approached and introduced himself in halting Thai. The doorman indicated he follow him into the club. The music grew louder as the sounds of the street outside diminished. The dark room had a purple hue created by the UV lighting that ran behind the mirrored bar. Matt followed the tight black t-shirt that struggled to stretch across the biceps of the man in front of him. His eyes were drawn to the view of lithe brown bodies twisting and bending around poles on small stages around the club. A throng of drooling middle aged men and curious wide eyed tourists circled each platform. The doorman led him to a back corner, set slightly higher than the rest of the floor, several tables with soft, leather chairs were gathered together, a respectful distance apart. Along the edge of the raised step a purple rope strung between brass poles gave a clear message that this was the VIP area. On seeing the doorman and Matt approaching a bouncer unhooked the rope and silently stood aside. Matt was struggling with the subdued lighting, the smoky atmosphere was stinging his bloodshot eyes. His head still thumped with the excesses of the previous night and he cursed himself for the solitary drinking session he had slipped into sitting on a stool at the hotel bar. He could make out three men clustered round a table in the corner, probably the only table unfussed by strippers. An older Thai man was sat in the middle, wearing a more formal, traditional high collar silk shirt, small yellow dragons weaved their way across the green silk and around the front fastenings. Probably in his fifties, his face was lined but his fleshy skin and well filled body suggested a life of leisure. His grey hair was Brylcreemed away from his temples, accentuating the eyebrows that had kept their dark colour. Leaning back in his chair he silently digested the conversation of the two men sat either side of him. One an attractive Westerner, early thirty something Matt guessed. Sandy hair flicked just to his shoulders, the whites of his blue eyes and perfectly straight teeth set against the deep bronze of his skin, the colour of a white man living in perpetual sunshine. He was talking excitedly with the air of a coke head, hand gestures accompanying his dialogue. His clothes were trendy, a designer t-shirt with a large punky emblem, possibly a shade too young for him. Matt couldn't help but feel the prickles of resentment. He was one of the cool kids that had always dismissed him. The other was a Thai guy, probably the same age but with a far more serious manner. Precisely cut black hair matching the colour of his t-shirt that was tucked neatly into a pair of dark jeans. One foot was resting on the opposite knee and Matt could just make out the sharply pointed toe and high heel of black leather cowboy boots. The doorman approached the cowboy and bending down whispered something in his ear. The Thai's eyes flickered over Matt. The Westerner, realising the attention had been diverted from him, turned his head to stare at this newcomer. The Thai guy then spoke to the older, fatter bloke in the middle. He nodded his head and then stood up, smiling at Matt and offering his hand.

"Good evening Mr Isaacs. It is a pleasure to meet you. I am Virote. Come, come, we will go through to my office."

Matt nodded dumbly and followed Mr Big through a side door at the end of the bar. He could feel the eyes of the cowboy burning into his back. The door opened into a brightly lit corridor at the end of which a staircase ran downwards, presumably to the cellar. The big man tapped a door on his left with the knuckle of his forefinger. It opened a crack and a young Asian guy stuck his face in the gap. On seeing the older man he stepped backwards opening the door enough to allow Virote and Matt through. Stepping into the large office space, Matt was first greeted with a long, black leather sofa that ran along the back wall. A young guy was slouched against the chrome arm, smoking. His floppy dark brown hair fell across his left eye, a faint scar running from his lower eyelid barely concealed. On seeing his boss he stood up quickly, the creases in his blue linen trousers unfolding, only his bare toes showing from underneath . Virote gave a small nod indicating he should sit back down. The scarred face threw a disarming grin at Matt who could only manage a one sided smile in response. His attention was being drawn towards a low guttural moaning, like the sound of a cow in distress. In the space between the sofa and the office desk a large Asian bloke, snake tattoos circled the backs of his hands and up under his shirt sleeved shirt. He seemed to be holding court in the centre of the room. His acne scarred face was shining under the brightness of the office lighting, a sheen of perspiration that he occasionally wiped with the back of his arm across his top lip. A ceiling fan above him rhythmically lifted the hair at the back of his neck, wet curls that gently bounced in the breeze. His short sleeved shirt was open at the neck, the clawed feet of a dragon tattoo curled up to his clavicles. His blue and cream paisley silk shirt was spotted with dark stains that ended in round crimson blobs on the tops of his white trainers. In front of him a man was tied to a gun metal chair. His spiny back was to Matt who could see the deep red sores the ties had sawn into his wrists. The man's head was slumped onto his bare chest, perspiration glued his hair into the hollows of his temples. The contours of his profile were angular, high cheek bones and a prominent nose. Matt couldn't quite place his ethnicity. The skin of his back looked soapy under the glare of the white light, his veins were pumped blue and green running down his forearms. In between the moans his breaths bubbled through liquid.

"Aah Mr Isaacs, you appear to have joined us at a delicate time. Would you rather wait in the bar?" The big man looked directly into Matt's expression, calculating every minor twitch. Matt wasn't the sharpest tool in the box but he understood the message.

"No, it's fine. Not a problem."

"Good. We have been very lucky this evening. We have been looking for this gentlemen for sometime. He seemed to be under the impression that he could rob me. Please take a seat and I will try and resolve this quickly." Virote walked behind the heavy wooden desk pulling his chair up and leaning both elbows on the table. His deeply lined face creased into a smile as he looked to the guy with the tattoos.

"Please continue"

Matt sank into the sofa next to the Thai fella who offered him a smoke. The tattooed guy was talking into the robber's ear. Matt couldn't understand what he was saying but his tone seemed to carry a million threats. The thin mouth sliced into an evil smile. A huge sob choked out of the robber's mouth, coughing then raked his lungs and a spatter of blood spayed onto the polished concrete floor in front of him. Virote curled his upper lip in disgust at the mess on his office floor. The tattooed guy was holding a slit throat razor in his right hand, the ivory handle almost pearlescent. He pressed it into the bend of the prisoner's left elbow, with a small push he began to draw it down the blokes arm, like a red pen leaving a trail behind it, it scored all the way to the man's wrists. The red line began to wobble and move as the blood rose out of the cut.

The tears and blood combined as the man choked and convulsed against his constraints. The torturer leant across the back of the chair and pointed the tip of the blade into the other elbow, the captive slumped, his damaged arms dangling against the hard metal. Another threat was spat into the side of the seated man's face, he leant far to his right, away from his captor and began to beg, Matt didn't understand the words but he could feel the rhythm in the man's whimpered prayers. The torturer grabbed the top of his prisoner's left ear and yanked it towards him, holding the head into his midriff. The blade pressed into the hard nobble of the man's skull. Matt watched the trickle of urine as it spread from the bottom of the right trouser leg, a puddle spreading around the legs of the chair. The torturer noticed his shoe now sitting in this wet substance. He cursed and drew the blade down the knobbly flesh behind the ear. It peeled away, it's rubbery texture holding it's shape even as it was held by the tattooed hand. A scream shrieked from the captive, stopped by more choking, bent over the blood running from the gaping hole of his flesh along the line of his chin, his feet twitching against the restraints around his ankles. The torturer threw the chewy piece of skin onto the floor behind him, landing just a couple of feet from where Matt was sitting. He stared at the distorted piece of flesh, how insignificant it now seemed.

The big fella said something to the torturer. He then smiled at Matt and indicated that they leave.

"Come now Mr Isaacs. I am done here, let us continue our evening in more pleasant surroundings."

Matt followed him, the thump of the bass jumping into his throat as they left the corridor and entered the dim, hot environment of the club. Matt felt a tingle in the pit of his belly, excitement quivering his bowels; he was in, he was on the up.

-8-

Guy

Guy's pencil shuffling along his notepad was the only sound in the grey cell. The small square window had not revealed the tiniest glimpse of blue all day and he felt as if he had been existing a few metres under a cloud. There had been no reprieve either, a short staffed Sunday meant they had been locked up for twenty four hours. He had become immune to the stale smell of his unwashed cellmate, his nose had given up continuing the lighter, shorter intakes and, accepting that there was no fresh air to be found, had resigned itself to breathing the thick atmosphere. He couldn't believe that someone could go so long without moving. Lying on his side, facing the wall, Badger had spent the entire weekend with his nose stuck in his book. How many times had he read that bloody thing? Although the occasional turning of a page confirmed his belief that the crumpled and filthy man on the bottom bunk was an incredibly slow reader. He had begun to resemble a rich person's hermit tucked away in some folly. His black beard was dense and tightly curled, a streak of white wove it's way up and under the waves of it's dark neighbours. His hair stood at crazy angles off his scalp, a permanently tussled, grease defining 'bed head'. The serious expression on his face deepened the lines running from his nose and around his mouth, a mouth which Guy struggled to see amongst the forest of hair on his top lip.

He wasn't quite sure how long this was going to go on for. He had seen him get low before but not for such a solid period. Was he going to snap out of it this time? Should he try and intervene? Truth was, there were times when he enjoyed the silence, when Badger was feeling good it was almost too much. The words would tumble from him, a cascade of poorly defined plans and torrential details about the butchery. His precious evenings could be completely suffocated by the animated jumble that filled the four small walls.

His mind completely distracted, he put his pencil down and twisted round in his chair. You had to feel sorry for him though, curled up in the foetal position, his eyes attached by invisible lines to the paperback resting in his hand. Surely he needed a break from it?

"Badger, hey Badger."

The head moved slowly round, a quizzical expression across his brow as if he was surprised anyone else was there.

"Take a break and let's have a game of cards."

The book was still in his hand as he straightened his body, the languid motion reminding Guy of a lizard at the beginning of the day, stiff before the sun's heat had penetrated the cold muscles. Both arms reached behind his head, the palms pressing on the wall as he let out a groan in a full length stretch.

"Dunno if I'm in the mood."

"Is the book a bit depressing for you mate?"

Badger sat up, swinging his legs to the floor. "It's not depressing, how can it be depressing? It's amazing what this guy knows, he really understands and he's not stupid, the things he does, you can really see where he's coming from."

Guy was puzzled "Do you mean the author or the main character?"

Badger pondered for a minute, Guy got the impression that it had only just occurred to him that they might not be one and the same.

"Um, I dunno, I just know that this bloke really understands."

"You identify with the book is that it?"

"Yeah, identify, definitely."

Guy quickly ran through his book memories. Wasn't this the one all about revenge on the father? The kid that was so screwed up he became a psychopath? Looking at the brooding figure sat in front of him the little finger of unease began to tap again.

"Yeah, I remember. The kid was treated very badly, real heartbreaking stuff, but he turned into a nasty piece of work."

Badger's brow tightened downwards, his dark eyes glittered with anger. "Wouldn't you though?" and his voice became louder, a coarse growl stirred deep in the throat "Wouldn't you fucking turn out that way? He had no choice, look at what they did to him. He had to fight for his life." His sentence broke with a tremble.

"Well, I think that's the skill of the author, to evoke such feeling in you."

Like a balloon with a gentle puncture Badger's body seemed to soften and reduce in size as the anger subsided.

"How's it going in the butchery? You haven't told me much for a while, are you still enjoying it?"

A smile closed the gap between his facial hair and his sideburns. "Yeah, I'm doing a lot of work on my own now, you know cutting all the meat for the prison."

"So I should be admiring your handiwork on my plate then?"

"Oh yeah, I'm getting really good. Fast you know, I reckon I'd be good at slaughtering too. I've been asking my mentor about it. It's all about keeping your tools really sharp and keeping yourself clean. I reckon it's what I'll be doing when I get out of here."

"Cool." Guy was pleased to see his old mate smiling again, he wasn't all that bad, jeez you could get a lot worse in the prison.

Over the next couple of months Guy watched with interest as their cell map became ever more colourful and confusing. Lines were drawn between markers and small notes had been stuck on various continents. When Badger wasn't around Guy had taken the opportunity to try and study the small yellow post-its in more detail but the childlike shorthand meant absolutely nothing to him and he couldn't be bothered to sit through Badger's rambling explanations. There had been a few more funny episodes when he seemed to lose his cellmate in some kind of crazy abyss but at the moment he seemed to be on a stable one.

Guy was dreaming into his latest hardback. Photographs of vineyards in the major wine growing regions interspersed the text. Lying down on his bunk, he held the book above him drinking in the double spread. Rows of vines carpeted the foreground, a cloudless blue sky rested on purple mountains. Closing his eyes he tried to imagine the gently scented clean air. He could almost hear the piercing monosyllabic calls of the birds of prey that would circle the wide expanses of land, gliding as their elegant wings caught the thermals that ran from the high ground. His nose began to detect an alien smell, not from within his inner world but something that pulled him back to the still air of his confined space. His eyes opened and his aching arms placed the large book down on his legs.

"I do believe I can smell the sweet fumes of a marijuana cigarette dear Watson."

A deep throated giggle shook the bunk.

"I'm celebrating."

"Oh, I'm always one for a party." And Guy jumped down from his bunk, sitting himself cross legged, at the end of Badgers bed. Badger was lying on his back and trying to avoid burning his chest as he held the glowing joint above him.

"You know that smoking dope, lying down, is seriously bad for your health. Under this chest hair I can reveal many scars from post-coital smoking."

Badger laughed as he stretched his arm across to Guy, the smoke exiting his nose in puffs with each chuckle. Guy took the joint and savoured the burn in his out of practice throat.

"Go on, why the celebration."

"I've got home leave."

"Well done mate, they won't trust me with any of that yet, reckon I'm too much of a flight risk. Can't say I blame them."

"Keep trying, they're pretty dumb. I've had it on loads of occasions and I've just pissed off. They've caught me an' all but it doesn't affect you re-applying and they just don't seem to keep records of it."

"Well, maybe I should." Keeping the last intake in his throat he bent forward to hand the joint back to Badger. "Fucking hell, that's not bad." Guy could feel his brain slowing and flopping at the sides, sensible conversation dropping off the edges.

"I know." And Badger let the smoke drift out from between his grinning teeth.

"So, you gonna bugger off then?"

"Yep, I reckon it's time. I can't handle being in here too long, does my nut in. I get funny thoughts you see, I call it my blackness. When it happens I just can't seem to shake it, reckon I get it from my old man. Anyhow, I've got stuff to do,

I need to get away from here, I can't bear this fucking place it's not good for me"

"Oh, that's a shame, I was really enjoying it!" both men spluttered with laughter, their bellies entering involuntary spasms.

Badger gained control "I'm leaving you the map man." Both heads turned to the blue and green poster on the wall, obliterated by post-its, hand drawn lines and different blobs of chewing gum and blu-tack.

Guy tried to straighten the corners of his mouth, willing his muscles to pull his face into an expression of serious gratitude. "I er, I don't know what to say," he noticed a twitch at the corner of Badgers mouth, "oh you bastard!" And both men were gripped in laughter again, struggling to catch their breath the tears began to form in the corners of their eyes.

"I'll send you a postcard." Silent wheezing accompanied the rocking bodies, Guy felt a tiny prickle in his gut as he realised his constant companion was leaving him. "I'm going to miss you," Badger looked up. "No, I'm serious man, I've got used to you."

Badgers giggles chugged slowly down to the occasional hiccup. "Thanks" and he smiled one of the warm, reassuring grins that always dissolved the reservations that Guy suffered. "I'd like to keep in contact, you could add my postcards to the map."

"Course."

Badger looked at him with earnest eyes "Maybe we could meet up when you get out, I'd love to come on your boat."

Guy quickly chewed through several thoughts before answering. It was one thing to be best buddies on the inside but did he really want the friendship of this disturbed man on the out? He visualised his usual group of friends and imagined their discomfort, Badger was hardly the laid back, sunny natured type. His conscience twisted, at the end of the day he had been a friend in here and if he were to ignore him on the outside it would be nothing more than snobbery, intellectual or otherwise. Something he despised his father for. His mouth began to part in response, just as the first word cracked in his throat, Badger jumped in; "I could be very useful you know, I've got loads of experience in the smuggling game."

Guy's shoulder's relaxed, "Ah mate, I'm not sure I'm going back into all that again. If I get caught they'll stick me away until I'm an old man" Badger's eyes started to slip, focusing on the scratchy woollen blanket of his bed "but look, I would love to meet up again and of course you could come on the boat. Keep writing and I'll know where you are."

The dark eyelashes rose and a gentle, dopey looking smile spread across Badger's face "Of course I will." Guy lowered his voice, mimicking the seriousness of his father "but, there is one condition."

A lopsided frown caused one of Badger's eyelids to drop, "what's that?"

"Why the fuck have I been calling you Badger for the last six months?"

"Oh, god, well, it's really stupid. I kind of picked it up in prison and so I've always used it when I'm inside, it's like my prison name you know?"

"Don't just give me that, there must be a reason behind it." Guy had twisted himself round, his head needing the support of the brick wall, his legs dangled off the edge of the bunk. He was feeling completely wrecked and was looking forward to closing his eyes and being told a story.

"Okay, well, I was going through one of my facial hair periods, beard an' all, and you know how that looks, all black with that bit of white. I was in an open prison and a load of fellas had stuff chucked over the fences for Christmas. Well one bloke I got quite friendly with; I had asked him if he'd knock off my missus new fella but he wasn't going for it; anyway, in his Christmas parcel was a jar of peaches in brandy. Well, no-one likes that stuff but he offered them to me and I thought, sod it, it's Christmas, they might be worth a try. Well, I was sat in my cell and going mad with boredom, excuse me," Badger leant over the edge of the bunk while he coughed. "God, I need a drink"

Guy opened his eyes. "Oh bollocks, you can't stop there" as he spoke he noticed the lack of saliva in his mouth, the words feeling sticky and difficult to form. "You're right, I'm parched too." He slid off the bunk, holding the metal bar of his bed, he pulled himself into a standing position. Taking a step towards the desk, the laughter began to bubble again, his legs felt like lead and his feet as huge as clowns. His wrist nearly gave way under the weight of the water jug and when he tried to pour it a jelly-like sensation flowed through his fingers. "Oh bollocks and bollocks" the water flowed too quickly from the jug, sploshing over the edge of the first tumbler. He picked up his notepad and moved it across to blot the mess, rather than soaking, it pushed the water off the table and onto his bare toes. "Oh bloody bollocks." Finally, with two shaky hands he managed to pass a beaker to Badger, who with a spine that was liquefied by marijuana, looked like a slinky unravelling from the top of the metal headrest, down to the where his toes met the bottom. Guy shoved the slack legs to one side and took up his original position leaning against the wall. "Go on."

"Well, there was these peaches and all looking golden and treacly in the brandy so I thought, just one might be nice, can't be that bad. Anyway, I was off my head and had forgotten that I was in full munchies, I ate the whole jar, god knows how many, five maybe, and then I drank the bloody juice. Course, being stoned an' all it just got all stuck in my beard and I wasn't feeling good. I tried to get up to get to the lav but I couldn't stand, I fell onto my knees and I just couldn't be arsed to try and get up again. My cellmate found me and got the attention of a few others. Well, they all took the right piss and one smart fella said it reminded him of a documentary he'd seen where these badgers had gotten drunk on a load of rotten fruit. So, Badger it was and Badger it stayed all the time I was inside. If I ever bump into anyone that knows me inside, that's what they call me."

Guy could not physically make a sound, the image in his head of the sticky black and white beard and the stupid bastard lying on the floor had been too much for his laughing muscles to keep pace. The tears streamed from his eyes, his stomach hurt more than he could ever remember. Finally, after several deliberate sucks at the air around him, he managed to speak. "You will always be Badger."

Like a drop of liquid mercury the disappointment was an invisible, internal coldness that came to rest in Badger's chest cavity.

-9-

Matthew

A couple of years later, sitting at a Singapore restaurant table he wondered at the purity of the seafood he had ordered. His table overlooked the Strait. The sun was slowly sinking into the sea, a shimmering halo surrounded it. Huge tankers and commercial fishing boats lined the horizon. Man made, polluting objects, black against the orange and pink sky. How clean was the sea really? Over-fished to feed this over-populated city. The East Coast promenade was a racing track of cyclists and power walkers. Office workers and families enjoying the cooler evening to get some exercise and sea air. A bowl of noodles was set down in front of him, shrimps, cuttlefish and crab nestled into the oily soup. He picked up the chop sticks, holding the bowl to his chin he ate with the dexterity of a local. He wondered at his image. After spending the last couple of years travelling Asia he hoped to convey the look of an interesting, sophisticated Westerner. His clothes were crumpled with the humidity but expensive.

Every suit custom made, his shoes soft beaten leather. He had no permanent home, no connection's, no responsibilities. He enjoyed the solace. There was just one thing missing, or possibly two things. He wondered what she was doing. How old would the child be now? He knew she would still be thinking of him. Impossible for her to forget him, she still belonged to him, even if that police bastard husband of hers was still around. She was the only woman for him, she was special, not like all the other sluts that put themselves out for him. Maybe it was time to risk travelling back to the UK. He'd had no problems using his passport all this time, no-one had ever picked up that he was wanted back in England. The remainder of his sentence was still outstanding. A greasy droplet of blackbean sauce ran down his chin, landing on the white linen shirt. Fuck, another shirt ruined. He watched a family along the boardwalk, the father pulling a child's trailer behind his bike. That's what he would do. It was time to go back. Tell her that he'd made it. He could even do a bit of work on the way.

Squashed into the toilet cubicle he placed his foot on top of the suitcase. Leaning forward he breathed out, relaxing the muscles of his anus. He blocked out the noises around him, anything that disturbed him would make the muscles clench and the whole process would become painful. He took the first bullet shaped package and began to slide it up his arse, smothered in Vaseline, it moved easily. He pushed it high enough that he couldn't detect it when the ring of muscle closed again. Good. Time for the next one. He leant over and breathed out again. The second one was more of a struggle, they were pretty long and hard and to sit two in the cavity without being aware of them, was always tricky. He stood up, allowing his bottom to come to rest naturally. He pulled his pants and trousers up and packed away the masking tape in his hand luggage. Just in case. On occasion he had removed the packages and strapped them under his bollocks. Nothing worse than losing $4000 down the airplane toilet. He unlocked the door and washed his hands before joining the check-in queue.

He picked at his food on the plane, just enough not to arouse suspicion. He was sat next to an older English woman, in her fifties he would guess. She smiled amiably at him when they took their seats, his next to the window, but had made no attempt at conversation since. She had her nose buried in a book most of the time. It suited him, he was beginning to feel uncomfortable and was trying all his usual relaxation attempts to distract himself. He had played music on the in-flight headphones, scoured the duty free magazine for trinkets to waste his money on and run through countless scenarios with Nieve. But it wasn't working, the second package had slipped and it sat at the entrance of his anus, ready to evacuate. There was nothing for it, the pressure couldn't be ignored any longer. He got up, excusing himself over the legs of his fellow passengers and locked himself in the lavatory. Sitting down on the toilet he cupped his hand and sure enough the hard little bullet emerged. It was still nicely intact, the copious wrapping in cling film held the white powder tightly. He ran a cross of masking tape along it and stuck it underneath his ball sack, close fitting underpants made it feel more secure.

Dirty Luggage

Over France now, just another hour and he would be facing the obstacle course of immigration and customs. It wouldn't be a problem, there was no reason for anyone to be suspicious of him. He couldn't stop the sweating though. The anticipation poured out of him, sticking his fringe to his forehead. Out of the corner of his eye he noticed the woman taking sideways glances at him. She looked cool, composed, not a strand of her grey hair was out of place. Immaculately combed into a bun her ears were exposed. Small diamond studs dragged her lobes downwards. He wondered if they were real, they certainly looked heavy enough. How tempting just to pull them out, a small split through her thin lobes, that would be all. She had bent over, pulling her handbag from under the seat in front, an ostentatious Louis Vuitton, no doubt bought in one of the cheaper Singapore designer outlets. She unzipped it, placing her book inside. He could see the matching purse, it looked fat, plenty of credit cards and cash. Mind you, if she was that flush she'd be sitting in first class surely?

The plane had started it's descent, he could see the familiar cliff faces of the South of England. No matter how long you left, it still felt like home. He had nothing to pack up, he had sat without entertainment for hours. As the plane bounced down at Heathrow the hard balls of anxiety bounced in Matt's throat.

The airport looked dirty and grey. Pale faces bustled around him, everyone in their own bubble. A respectful distance between all the travellers as they patiently waited for their luggage to mysteriously appear on the carousel. With each flap of the rubber curtain Matt prayed he would see his hard burgundy suitcase. He tried to control his twitching fingers, they were desperate to pull the shirt away from his sticky back. He kept reminding himself to resist it, October in London, there was no excuse to be hot. When he saw the suitcase appear on the other side of the carousel he rooted his feet to the spot, no need to rush. It slowly trundled towards him and he finally stepped up and pulled it from the conveyor belt. He tipped it onto a corner and pulled it by the loose handle, it's small wheels clattering along on the hard floor.

Immigration next. He held his passport in his hand, nothing to worry about.

Ian Terrent had worked for immigration for twelve years. He was good, he knew all the subtle signs, no brick through a window was needed. In between looking down at each proffered passport he would raise his eyes above the passengers directly in front of him and scan the approaching travellers, weaving their way around the ropes and metal poles. The man with the hard, red suitcase was interesting. He looked dishevelled. Not that it meant much in an airport, but he looked sweaty and dishevelled. There was a stiffness in his movements that couldn't be excused by old age. He wasn't looking up an awful lot. Officer Terrent continued to smile and scan the passports offered up to him but kept his eye on the man as he slowly snaked his way towards his desk.

Matt stood behind the yellow line. He was next. Okay, cool, just a normal traveller, just like all the other times. Except now he was in England. Now he would be looked at by fellow Westerners who would find it easier to judge and assess him. The young family in front of him was finished.

He had chosen to queue up behind them, hoping that the annoyance of a crying toddler would detract attention from him.

He looked at the officer, in his forties, salt and pepper grey at the temples, a chiselled face hinting at a high level of personal fitness. Clean shaven and sharp eyed. Matt held his gaze in what he hoped was a relaxed, confident and friendly manner. The officer took his passport, tapping into a computer as he spoke. "Good afternoon sir. Where have you travelled from?"

"Singapore."

"And what was the nature of your trip?"

"Business and pleasure. I have a friend over there, I'm deciding whether to move permanently."

"Oh yes? And what is the nature of your business?"

"I'm in the antiques trade."

"Uh huh" Ian Terrent was looking at the screen in front of him. He just knew there was something. "I'm sorry sir but I'll need you to accompany a colleague of mine." Matt became aware of the presence of another man standing behind the immigration officer. Graham Roberts was older and broad, a soft paunch lay over the heavy leather belt. He was wearing a full uniform as opposed to the slightly more relaxed short sleeved shirt of the man at the desk.

The sweat became cool on Matt's skin, the bright lights of the hall began to swim.

"What's the problem?" He could only manage a whisper.

"Well, let's take one step at a time. My colleague will explain."

Matt looked up at the larger man beside him. "Mr Isaacs, there is a warrant outstanding for your arrest. You will come with me to an interview room where we will be able make some enquiries."

Fucking hell, fuck, fuck, fuck. The desire to escape was tugging at his reflexes. He scanned the room, officers everywhere. He had to get rid of the gear.

"I really need the toilet."

Graham Roberts looked at Ian Tremmen, both men smiled.

"Not a problem sir, there is a toilet in the custody suite."

Matt allowed himself to be led by the crook of his arm to an entranceway behind the line of desks. A whole array of offices, and glass walled waiting rooms greeted him. He was guided to a small office at the far end of the corridor. Graham Roberts opened the door.

"Please take a seat Mr Isaacs" Matt looked at the room, white and sanitary. An empty chair sat alongside a surgical bed surrounded by a green curtain. "You'll need to give us ten minutes to get the toilet ready, but first we will be conducting a strip search."

The smell of disinfectant was overpowering, Matt's empty stomach turned over, feeling light headed he sank onto the chair, the hard bullet pressed against his bruised perineum.

-10-

Guy

He'd kept his nose as clean as he could. Of course there'd been the odd hiccup but they understood that, you couldn't live amongst a bunch of criminals and never run into any trouble. Now was as good a time as any, the allocation officer was standing in front of the mirror puffing through sets of bicep curls, a smoker's wheeze at the edge of his deeper breaths. Even when pink with heat, Guy couldn't help but notice the faint grey shadow across his face, like a cancer sufferer before they're aware the disease is living in them. Beads of sweat gathered in tiny droplets on his bald head before running along the creases above his ears. He guessed he could feel the trickle for he stopped to wipe a hand towel across the back of his neck. Guy finished wiping the treadmill display and approached the resting officer.

"Would you like me to spot you on the bench press?"

"Cheers Guy."

Guy moved the bench into the middle of the free weights mat and began loading up two bar with free weights. The officer lay his towel across the bench before lying down, his legs bent and both his feet resting on the end. "How's it going?"

"No too bad guv, starting to wish for a change though, feel I could be achieving a lot more with my time."

"Oh yeah, I think I might know where you're coming from."

Guy placed the heavier bar onto the brackets above the officer's head. "It's just that I would like to gain more work experience before I leave the system. I've done my best to study here but there's a lot more opportunity if I can get to an open prison."

The officer picked up the bar and proceeded to puff out several reps, Guy kept his hand supporting the middle, helping to place it back onto the brackets.

"I hear you Guy, I hear you, but you know there are a lot of people in the same situation and everyone wants it just as much. How do I choose who to give the placements too, there's not many that come up."

The officer took his eyes off the weights for a fraction of a second, looking straight into Guy's. The penny dropped.

"I'll see what I can do guv."

Another call to dad. Guy stood in front of the phone box on the landing, staring at the black handset. He ran through the probable conversation in his head, wanting to make sure he had thought of as many different responses before he had his father's dominant voice on the line. A thin youngster slunk up to him.

"Are you finished mate?" Guy looked into the sunken face. "I haven't used it yet, I'm not ready, you go ahead."

The kid smiled, exposing yellow teeth, the gums already receding. "I know, it's difficult coming up with a new one eh?" Guy didn't respond, the kid was obviously about to use a line on some poor desperate relative to try and wangle some money for gear. He took a step away, leaning on the balcony as he earwigged on the whining voice.

"I know nan, I know but he say's he's gonna have me……..I know I told him, I tried……..You should see what they do to you nan………….It's bad, really bad…………………..Once I'm out of here……………..Never again, no……………you're an angel, honestly nan if I didn't have you……….oh yeah, I'd be dead right now……………..the usual unless you can spare any……….everything helps, it makes it easier for me you know…………yeah nan, love you too.

The handset was set back down and the sickly face turned to him. "All yours mate."

Guy stepped forward, he lifted the handset and slid the phonecard into the telephone. He gazed out at the landing while he listened to the ringing tone. The phone suddenly went dead, shit had they hung up on him? He turned from his view over the balcony to the telephone fixed on the wall. A large hand, a smudged green tattoo on each knuckle, was resting on the phone cradle. He followed the arm up to it's owner, registering more hand drawn tattoos, his eyes fell upon the square jaw of the Slasher, a well-known bully amongst the inmates. His small eyes sat closely above a nose that seemed devoid of any spine, flattened into a rubbery hump no doubt by countless breaks. The smile was more of a sneer.

"All right Captain. Reckoned you wouldn't mind if I used your phone card for a bit."

Guy wanted to just nod his head and move quietly away from the callous psycho but was determined to show a bit of face.

"Actually, I would mind, I'm sorry mate but that call was very important to me."

"Are you suggesting-" the Slasher drew his gravelley voice into a slow drawl, mimicking Guy's middle class accent "-that my phone call is less important than yours?"

Guy knew he had to tread carefully, the Slasher thrived on violence, it was a form of expression and any outlet, any excuse gave him much delight. Guy had witnessed his handiwork when stuck in the corner of the shower block before.

"No, but letting me make my call could serve us both." Slasher stared at Guy, giving himself a moment to let his mind catch up with his instincts.

"What you got in mind?"

"Do you like the horses?"

"I'm more of a dogs man but go on."

"I have an extremely reliable source on the tracks, in fact, his tips are the best you will ever get." Guy kept his face fixed in an expression of complete neutrality.

"All right, you got me interested but if I find out you're taking me for a cunt you're gonna find yourself in the hospital ward."

Slasher leant against the brick wall and lifted his hand from the cradle of the handset. The dial tone sprung back into life. Somehow Guy needed to get him away from the phone, he didn't want him to hear who he was talking to.

"Look, I'm sorry mate but I really need some privacy, this phone call is not going to work like this."

The Slasher grabbed a handful of Guy's t-shirt, yanking a handful of his chest hair with it. Pulling Guy's face close to his own, the smell of stale tobacco and cheap after shave was so overpowering Guy struggled to keep his nose from wrinkling shut in disgust. "Are you fucking around with me rich boy? Are you taking me for a wanker?"

Guy's resolve began to wither, his knees had definitely given way and he loathed himself for it. If he replied immediately there was a good chance his voice would break into a squeak and he couldn't bear it. Staring into the angry, beady eyes, he swallowed before answering.

"Look mate, I really don't mean any disrespect and I'm sorry if that's how it came across, but this phone call is a bit delicate, if I'm going to get the information I need I've got to do a lot of sweet talking first and if I'm being totally honest I find it hard to do, and a bit embarrassing if someone's listening."

He felt the grip loosening and his breath slowly drew out. A sly chuckle accompanied a painful dig in the ribs by his elbow, "Oh I get it, you got a chat up a bird right?"

"Uh huh."

"Alright."

The Slasher walked slowly backwards, eyes on Guy the whole time, until he was at the end of the landing leaning into the corner.

Guy cursed himself, as if this phone call wasn't hard enough he now had added pressure. With an imperceptible tremor he picked up the handset and started again.

"Hello?"

"Mum, mum it's me, Guy"

"Oh darling, how are you? Are you alright? How are things?"

"I'm okay mum but I need to talk to dad again."

His mum's voice dropped into a conspiratorial whisper, "oh, I don't think that's a good idea at the moment darling, he's got people round and he's not had the best day."

"Mum this is really important. I've got a serious chance of being placed in an open prison, it means I'll be allowed out on a daily basis, I can go to work everyday, we can meet up without you ever having to step inside prison walls again."

Her voice rose in excitement, "oh that's wonderful, truly wonderful, but how can dad help?"

"I need a really good one mum, the allocation officer is one of dad's followers and if I can give him something then I know he'll do me a favour and put me up for it."

"Let me get dad."

In the moments silence Guy stole a glance to his watcher. The eyes had not left him, he knew his every movement was being scrutinised, he had to come up with the goods.

His father's deep voice punctuated his thoughts "Guy."

"Dad."

"Your mother's told me you need another favour."

"Yes, I'm sorry, but this is really important, look I didn't want to frighten mum but I've got an added reason to ask as well. I need it for the allocation officer to get me into an open prison and I've now got a neurotic, weapon loving gorilla on my back as well."

There was a moment's pause and when his father answered Guy was ashamed to hear the tears in the usually stern voice. "Okay son, have you got something to write on?"

"Yes, thank you dad."

Guy scribbled the information out twice and tore the bottom half off. He walked up to Slasher and keeping his arm down, discreetly passed the folded piece of paper into the rough palm.

"Let's hope for a bit of luck eh?" And the sneering mouth opened into a laugh showing off a golden molar.

Guy sang Little China Girl loudly and out of tune as he packed his box.

"Give it a fucking rest mate" his new cellmate, an ex-forces, grizzled man in his fifties growled from the bottom bunk.

Guy laughed, it felt so damn good to be getting out of this concrete box. He was moving to an open prison that looked more like Butlins than a place of punishment or, he grinned to himself, maybe that was the punishment. "I think that's it, I'm all done."

The cynical old voice barked at him again "What about that bloody thing? I don't want that shit left here."

Guy turned to Badger's map, one postcard so far from the states "Oh, that." He peeled the paper from the blu-tack and squidged the four small dots into a ball. "Well, I'll leave the blu-tack but I'll get rid of this." He folded up the crazy poster and placed it in the bin, he wasn't going to cart that load of rubbish around.

-11-

Matthew

He walked up the narrow path. Not much had changed, the grass in the front garden was still slightly longer than the neighbours, the borders boasted fewer flowers and no hanging basket dangled from the iron hook next to the front door. The door colour had changed though, the bizarre fuschia pink that she had loved in the eighties had been replaced by a more subdued sage green. Brass ironmongery gave the little terraced house a touch more class than it had before. Just as he reached the door, his arm stretching towards the doorbell, she appeared. Holding the door wide open, her heavy figure filled the frame.

He gave her his biggest toothy smile "Hello mum."

"So they let you out again. Stupid bastards, I told them an' all, I warned 'em you'd just bugger off again. Well, I guess you better come in then."

She turned her back to him and after closing the door, he followed her into the lounge. She sat on one of the velour armchairs. The raised green foliage pattern of the seat was worn flat and the velvet on the arms was thin underneath her nervous tapping fingers. Her apple shaped body fitted snugly, both legs touching the sides. Her knees were slightly apart, causing her blue knitted jersey dress to rise onto her thighs. Matt avoided looking at the tunnel of white fat that ran to his mother's huge briefs. She puffed as she leant sideways to reach a packet of fags on the table beside her. She pulled a cigarette out with her teeth offering the packet to him.

"No thanks mum, I'm trying to give up."

"Huh, when did you get so bleedin' high and mighty"

She eyed her son suspiciously. He had changed again. This time there was a new darkness in his eyes that unsettled her. Shadows of his father seemed to flicker across the brown circles like clouds scudding across the sky. A thin, cold needle of fear punctured her chest cavity.

Matthew, on the other hand, was feeling comfortable, superior even as he scanned the modest room. The glass fronted wall cabinet still contained the same depressing collection of Royal Doulton figurines, a naff ensemble ordered from the back of Sunday supplements. His mother's pride and joy, carefully dusted and then enclosed behind the sliding, locking, glass doors, who the bloody hell was going to steal them? The house itself was still, the windows hadn't yet been opened and the stale air held aromas of cigarettes and cooking fat. The muscles in his bottom twitched as the cloying atmosphere began to induce feelings of claustrophobia.

"I'm going to join Nieve mum, she's back in Mexico, but I need some help to get there."

"What bloody help do you think I can give you?" Her mouth pursed as she took another drag of the heavy, blue smoked cigarette.

"Anything mum, the little girl needs a dad. She's your granddaughter too."

"Do I ever get to see her? No. Never even met her, as far as I know, she's not even yours, so what the hell are you bothering with her for."

"She's mine mum."

Sometimes June Isaacs felt totally alien to her son. As she watched the feverish glint develop in his eyes she could only respond to his outward demands, although she had given birth to this person she had no idea what went on in his head, maybe it was better if he went. With distance between them she could switch herself off, whatever he did was his business and he was well away from her. Serves the bleeding authorities right, stupid bastards for keep trusting him. How many times had he bunked off when he was supposed to be on home leave? She couldn't even remember anymore. Best that he was gone all round.

"Get me my handbag; on the kitchen top."

Walking through to the small kitchen, Matthew felt like a little boy again. The yellow paint had dulled to a nicotine colour but the work tops and cupboards were still spotless, only the grease spatters from her high fat breakfast remained on the gas hob. Knowing mum, she'd be wiping that down before lunchtime. He wondered that she never noticed the smell though. This house had always stunk to him. Looking through the window his eyes focused on the back fence. It had been creosoted over the years, planks now leaned at dodgy angles leaving small gaps that people could peer through from the back alley. He remembered the neighbour's cat that had always sat on the top, like a sentry. Crazy things cats, you couldn't believe they could sit on something so narrow. He had a memory of it freaking out his mum one day, her screaming at it or something, but he couldn't quite formulate the whole picture. Was it that day? Matthew shrugged it off, better off not going there. Picking up his mum's fake Louis Vuitton he trudged back to the lounge.

"Here you go mum."

She pulled out her purse, a screwed up tissue landing on the floor. "I 'aven't got much."

"S'alright mum."

"Here." She passed him two hundred pounds. Matthew was surprised she had that much cash on her.

"Don't look so bleedin' shocked. Some of us work hard you know. Just take it and go, and don't ask for anymore."

June watched the broad back of her son walking down the front path and then folding himself to fit into a small hatchback; must be a rental car. It's tinny engine started first time and accelerated in bursts down the road. June pulled out another cigarette, let the bloody Diego deal with him.

Sunk into the blue and orange static fuzz of a window seat on the London train, Matt's eyes stared blankly through the glass. There was absolutely nothing he could do to turn the corners of his mouth up. Like the tragic mask of a sad clown he felt invisible weights pulling his expression lower and lower. A sticky cobweb of sadness lay upon him and he felt lonely, he could have been surrounded by a million loving arms and he would still feel lonely. There was an empty space in his soul, black, sometimes it felt like he was dead. Nothing touched him anymore, numb and still, like the surface of a deep pond. The occasional emotion would send a ripple across his mind again, a flickering light when his senses rose, fizzing briefly before the shadow crept across. He could still picture her face clearly, like a snapshot filed in the annals of his brain, it was always the same, the long black hair forever captured waving in the breeze, strands catching in the corners of her mouth, that wide, full mouth, the soft lips that had brushed his body, pressed against him, loved him. And they would again, of that he was sure. His heart palpitated in reply, drawing his consciousness back to the physical world, the soft, square of folded paper between his thumb and forefinger. Her letter, he had read and re-read it, the paper beginning to crumble along the folds. She had left the police officer, she didn't really say why but he knew it was because she still loved him. She had gone back to Mexico with the little girl, his little girl otherwise why would the copper let her go? He could feel her waiting for him, her voice pulling inside his head, drawing him to Mexico. He would join them and they would become a family. His eyes slid from the green whirl and bump of trees speeding past the glass and to the passenger sat across from him. Trying to protect her personal bubble of space she had chosen to sit diagonally opposite, her legs crossed and pointing outwards to the aisle. A pointy white elbow rested on the arm of the seat, a paperback held amongst the slender fingers. He guessed she was mid twenties, although her serious expression characterised an old spinster, her skin was smooth with a gentle blush over cheeks that hadn't yet felt the sucking pull of being too slim. Her ash blonde hair was severely combed away from her face and into a ponytail, the band that held it simple black reflecting the tight pencil skirt that her calves just managed to squeeze from. Her eyes were glued to the pages in front of her but the bobbing motion of her top foot conveyed a different message to him. She was aware that he was studying her, he knew that her eyes desperately wanted to slide sideways to look at him but were afraid that he would catch her. Although she looked all hoity toity her faux leather briefcase and synthetic court shoes gave her away. He turned back to the window, she wasn't worth anything.

The train swept closer to London, rows of terraces lined the railway track, Matt began to enjoy the glimpses into the backs of these people's lives. The dirty, tawdry side they tucked away from the front. Dustbins, washing flapping on slack lines, rusty bikes and deflated, algae covered paddling pools. They were all the same. They all thought they were unique, individual and special but, they were all the same, members of an enormous herd.

The train began to stop more often, swarms surged towards the doors, filing along the carriages searching for an unoccupied seat. Matt bumped his bottom closer to the window as an overweight, red faced business man squeezed into the space beside him, a small trickle of sweat ran through the thinning grey hair at his temples. As he loosened his tie Matt noticed the heavy watch that just fell over the edge of the cuffs of the silky looking white shirt. Interesting. He continued to study his subject, enjoying the openness of his stare. The bloke was too busy faffing around, juggling a newspaper, briefcase and some obviously very pressing paperwork, to notice the attention Matt was giving him. He had balanced the briefcase on his lap and was using it as a desk for his documents. A gold Mont Blanc pen rested loosely in his right hand, occasionally circling something in the text. Yep, he was worth something. The emptiness of Matt's wallet gnawed at him, he needed money desperately if he was gonna get away from here. Mum's money was just enough to pay for travel and food but it would hardly get him far. Matt cleared his throat.

"Have you finished with your paper?"

The man turned to him, the blue of his eyes was so weak they were almost opalescent. His eyebrows were slightly raised in a mildly startled expression.

"I'm sorry, pardon?"

"Your newspaper, have you finished with it?" Matt nodded down at the crinkled broadsheet sandwiched between the two men.

The heavy wrinkled skin almost blanketed his eyes as he smiled revealing the dehydrated white goo at the corners of his mouth "Oh yes, of course, please help yourself" and he leaned slightly away allowing Matt to easily pull the paper from between them.

It was a struggle to read it. Having been well thumbed during the course of the day the paper had lost any crispness and the corners flapped over softly. It needed to be folded and that required arm space. Matt pressed himself into the corner of the seat, his head leaning on the cool glass of the window as he shook the loose paper out and confidently arranged it into a neat square. He then settled back into his seat and stared at the black and white print of the business pages while he had a think about what to do. The girl would have overheard everything of course but she hadn't really ever looked at him. She'd been so desperate not to catch his eye or risk conversation that she had kept her beaky little nose stuck into her book. He glanced above him. His small rucksack was on the wire rack over the seats, he hadn't taken anything out so he was ready to pick it up and jump off the train whenever he needed. He wondered how far this guy was going, his original intention was to hop off at one of the main junctions and work his way to the airport but it was pointless without some money behind him. The train deposited passengers at two more stops before there was any sign of the guy packing up beside him and then, the documents began to get shuffled into a pile and the briefcase was clicked open. Matt's insides sparked into painful, adrenalin ridden pangs. He breathed slowly outwards, hoping to calm the pulse that threatened to reveal itself in the sweat prickling on his forehead. The clattering of the train began to slow into more rhythmic rolling beats as it approached the next suburb. Matt had been semi-conscious of the more mature trees and the generous park space that had broken up the squares of detached houses. He stood up and lifted his pack off the metal shelf, resting it on his lap as he sat down. He pushed the newspaper to the edge of the seat beside the window, he didn't want to deal with that again. At the first glimpse of the concrete ramp of the station Matt stood up, the guy took the cue and stood up too, moving out of the way and towards the doors at the end of their carriage. Following the creased suit jacket to the end of the aisle Matt cooled. Like the shallow end of a wave, the chilled feeling covered his emotions, his brain sharpening, ready to respond appropriately to whatever unplanned conversation or position it found itself in. There were a couple of people ahead of them lining up at the door, Matt braced his hand on the back of an occupied seat, not wanting to bump into his target when the train jolted to a stop. The guy moved slowly, his large frame seemed uncomfortable as he stepped down onto the platform. Matt had to adjust his pace to maintain his distance behind him, each metre was another moment of planning, precious time to observe and then make the right decisions. They turned off the bustling platform and into the cool interior of the station. The tiled floors conveyed the sounds of high heels, squeaking trainers and the occasional running footsteps of someone desperate not to miss their train. They passed the ticket booths on their right, Matt enjoying the weaving, erratic movements of the crowds to disappear into. He passed through the large open entranceway and into the muggy heat outside. Several steps led down to the road, Matt weaved his way through a straggly group of students sitting on the warm concrete. He then crossed the taxi bay and the wider turning circle before entering the cheaply fenced confines of the station car park. Perfect. If the guy hadn't left a car here then he would have to change tack. The heavily set man squeezed sideways between a dark blue BMW and a bright red Fiesta. Matt glided quickly up to the car next in line to the Fiesta, relieved to find it a respectable saloon, the kind of car that said 'I am a completely boring member of this tribe. I have two children, a soppy

Labrador and a wife that may work part time.' Standing at the drivers door he fumbled in his rucksack.

"Oh for Gods sake," he spoke loudly, using his best middle class, southern accent. He looked over his shoulder. The bloke was hanging his jacket on the hook behind the drivers seat, good, he still had an audience. He rummaged in his bag again, peering into the squashed clothes. "Bloody hell," this time his voice was deeper, a well pronounced growl in his throat. Looking to the sky he let out a loud sigh and then turned to his victim. Calling across the roof of the Fiesta, "excuse me?" Nothing, bollocks the guy was just about to fold himself into the drivers seat. He ran around the back of the Fiesta and approached the open door of the BMW. Leaning down he faced the puffy pink cheeks and damp hair of his fellow passenger. "I'm so sorry to trouble you but I've lost my car keys."

"Oh really?" Both legs came out from under the steering column and twisted to face Matt.

"Yes, and the really awful thing is that my wallet is missing too. I hate to say it but I've got a horrible feeling someone must have nicked them, I just can't understand how I could lose both things."

"No, that's a real bother isn't it. I'm sorry about that, you'll need to report it." Matt felt his prey edging away from him. He needed to pursue this and pretty quickly before there was any chance of someone else becoming involved.

"Yes, I certainly will. Could I be a real pain and ask where you'll be driving to?"

"Oh, um," Roger Stanton tried to assess his instincts and the physical appearance of the man in front of him. He seemed harmless enough, he certainly wasn't rough looking and he spoke very gently.

"I know it's a bit of an ask but I really must try and make tracks somehow, my wife will end up giving my dinner to the dog." Matt laughed and luckily the other bloke laughed with him. A little voice inside Roger told him not to be so stupid, the world was not full of bad people, the majority were perfectly ordinary human beings and why the hell shouldn't he take the opportunity to help someone out, he'd had a fucking awful day at work most of which he'd felt had been bad karma, maybe this was his chance to re-address the balance.

"Well, I'm going to the Woodcote Estate, is that any help?"

"Oh that would be perfect, you could drop me at the entrance and I can walk the rest of the way."

As Matt climbed into the passenger seat he threw his rucksack on top of the brief case at the back of the car, as he leaned across he eyed the heavy bulge of a wallet peeping from the top of the jacket pocket. Easy.

A pungent air freshener dangling from the rear view mirror invaded Matt's nostrils, he cracked open his window, enjoying the movement of his hair lifting from the nape of his neck. A country and western jangle suddenly blared from the stereo as Roger started the engine.

"Oh, I'm sorry, a little indulgence of mine." He chuckled nervously as he turned the volume down.

"That's alright, I don't mind a bit of music variety. Would you like a Polo?" Matt untwisted the small tube of mints, turning down the foil. "I don't even know your name!"

"Oh of course, Roger, and you?"

"Michael, call me Mike."

"Well thank you for the mint Mike. Have you been following the golf?"

"A little." Matt allowed his back to rest into the soft grey leather seat as he found warmth and banter enough to keep the conversation flowing. Actually, he really didn't need to stay much longer. A set of traffic lights was the sign he was waiting for.

"You know Roger, it's actually going to be easier if I jump out here." A look of surprise and then relief crossed the wobbly jowled face. "Oh, okay."

Swiftly Matt leant between the two front seats, grabbing his rucksack with his right hand and the wallet with his left. As he brought the rucksack through to the front he concealed the wallet behind it. "Well, many thanks Roger, it's been a pleasure." And just as the lights turned to green he slammed the passenger door shut, standing on the pavement, waved to the slow moving BMW as it continued to crawl through the backed up traffic. Fan bloody tastic. Matt grinned to himself, he just needed to find somewhere he could sit down and have a good look at his prize.

A bus shelter offered a bench and a rubbish bin, the two things Matt needed. Sitting down he pulled out the worn brown leather wallet. By the way it sat half open he knew it would be filled with crap, obviously someone who kept the receipts to everything. Sure enough, the curled edges of small squares of paper fought to stay inside one of the larger compartments but, to Matt's delight, there was also a large quantity of cash. He pulled it from the wallet like a bunch of documents from an envelope and folded it in half, stuffing the roll into the back pocket of his jeans. Now the cards. Three credit cards, two gold and one platinum. He stood up to slip them into the tighter pocket at the front of his jeans, enjoying the dig of their corners into his leg as he sat back down. The rest of the wallet was full of useful but worthless rubbish. Library card, a crumpled drivers license; no good to him because of the age of the fella, business cards, video rental. The gym membership made him snort. How many of these fat fuckers did he find with top of the range gym membership?

With a casual glance around him, he chucked the wallet and the remaining contents into the rubbish bin before hitching his rucksack onto his back and walking in the direction of the town centre sign he had spotted not so long ago.

The jewellers shop was in the middle of the pedestrianised high street, it's Rolex flag flickering above the shop fronts, his heart skipped a beat as the tingle of spending this blokes money spread through his extremities. As he walked past the full length window of a toy store it struck him that his appearance might be at odds with his spending power. He tried to steal surreptitious glances of his reflection and came to the conclusion that his jeans were too old and unfashionable and his scuffed white trainers were definitely not in keeping with the high value items he intended buying. He moved to the centre of the wide brick path, avoiding the window of the jewellers, he needed to find a menswear store first. As he moved away from the chain stores and burger joints, more independent boutiques were clustered together. A billboard, stark white with black mock handwriting was placed on the street outside a store. Underneath the modern and chic logo a list of designer names attempted to impress. Perfect. He felt relaxed and happy, the store smelt of success, solid wood floor, polished to a beautiful sheen, every garment hung with plenty of space between it and it's neighbour. He could just visualise the boutique paper bag that would be swinging from his hand in half an hour, he may even buy a few silk shirts, it was always extra nice when something was boxed. Starting at the front he eyed the chrome rails with slow, casual indifference. He knew the sales assistant was watching him, a young bloke, his hair all slicked back and looking far too smooth in a grey suit with pink shirt. He hoped the fella noticed how he paid no interest in the price tags, he would surprise their stuck up opinions when they saw how much he was going to spend. Who did these people think they were anyway? Definitely no better than him. The shop was quiet, there was only the low conversation of another customer being served at the changing rooms, every now and then a loud guffaw would attract Matt's attention. The assistant was holding up two sweaters in front of a well built guy, probably around forty, his hair was still ultra blonde. He was standing outside his changing room, completely shirtless, the curtain of his booth left open. He had a sportsmans physique, fit and strong without any of the over trained pumped look so common in the prisons. To Matt's horror, he caught him looking and flashed a huge grin, teeth far too white to be natural. Matt looked down, staring at the navy blue Armani sweater swinging in his hand. He wasn't going to risk going to the changing room now, the bloke looked half queer and he sure as hell wasn't like that. Keeping his back to the shop, Matt continued to work round the rails. He could hear the exchange at the till. The queer bloke had a strong accent, possibly German; in response to all the sales assistant's thank yous and have a nice days, he would reply ya. Matt was conscious that he had spent far too long in here. He was just going to buy the stuff without trying anything on, it didn't bloody matter anyway. His right palm was full of hanger hooks, looking down he counted the chrome heads, eight items, that was good enough. As he turned towards the till the tall, blonde customer turned away from it, both men were caught in front of one another.

"Ah excuse me." The loud voice boomed at Matt, the toothy smile flashing at him. Clear blue eyes, deep as the Mediterranean, stared into his. He could feel a flush begin to finger it's way up his neck. He was not going to reply to the queer, he held his gaze but kept his mouth closed.

"You have much shopping ya, is good fun."

Matt's stomach clenched itself into a fist. Couldn't this guy get the message? He tried taking a step to his right to pass the enormous presence. Just as he began to transfer his weight onto his right foot, the blue eyed face leant across, blocking Matt's vision. The full, smiling mouth then moved closer to his left ear and a hideous whisper tickled his hair.

"Don't be shy ya." And the face appeared in front of him again, Matt followed the movement of the blokes left eye as the lid moved downwards in a very definite wink. If he wasn't in such a public place, about to use a stolen credit card, his fist would have slammed into the blokes jaw, how he would love to smash those perfect fucking teeth. He struggled to control the rage inside him as he stepped up to the cashiers desk. His aching arm shook as he relieved it of it's load, dumping the garments on the glass top. The reptilian assistant sneered into a smile.

"You don't wish to try these on sir?"

"No thank you."

"In a bit of a rush are we?" There was a barely concealed smirk behind the comment. Matt glared into the slimey face, he was accusing him of being a poof.

"No."

The clothes were folded and the long, talon like fingers wafted tissue paper around, occasionally wrapping crease prone garments with it. The piles were slipped into two enormous glossy bags, twisted black rope for handles. Matt breathed a sigh of relief, after all that, he was finally going to get what he came for.

"And how are you paying?"

Matt brought out the platinum card. As it slipped through the machine Matt could not will his breath to leave his body. The gadget emitted a small beep and the reptile's smooth forehead crinkled into a frown. "I'm sorry sir, I just need to phone the bank."

That was it, the bastard had already reported it stolen, he had to get out of here now.

"You know, I'm in too much of a hurry for all this. I was hoping a client had cleared their account with me by now but obviously not, I'll need to get it sorted." Matt turned from the cashier and looked straight ahead at the open door.

"Sir, sir, I'm sorry but you need to stay." Matt didn't respond. In several ultra long strides he was out into the dusky street. He needed to disappear. The shops were beginning to close up, shutters were being pulled down and members of staff hanging around outside while alarms were set. He scanned the high street looking for an escape. Few shoppers were left and amongst them a tall, blonde head stood out. His back was to Matt and he was already halfway along the brick street before it met a busy road. Something was coming to him, the stirrings of an idea. He walked briskly towards the broad figure, concentrating on the rhythmic swinging of the man's shopping bag while he waited for his mind to throw the ball his way. He got it.

He pulled alongside him and stretched his cheeks into a smile, "Hi!"

The tall German looked to the voice that had suddenly appeared next to him. Recognition flicked across his eyes and then, when he noticed the arm brushing against his, delight.

"Hello shy boy."

"Maybe you got me wrong, I'm just not a very public person."

"Oh no well neither am I, I have a little apartment along the road here. Very convenient, just quick holiday rent while I work here."

The acids churned in Matt's stomach but he managed to increase his smile, "okay."

The kitchen was small, he could touch both sides if he stretched his arms, in fact the whole place was small, he could hear the disgusting bastard on the floorboards above his head. He had gone upstairs to change out of his suit but the sound of running water suggested he was washing as well. Sitting on the mock granite worktop was a wooden knife block. Several slots were empty except the two at the top, the ones bearing the longest knives. Constantly sliding his eyes to the door and his ears straining to follow the noise upstairs, Matt pulled the first one out. With a reassuring, smooth movement a heavy salad chopper revealed it's wide, steel blade. Matt wasn't so sure it was an appropriate choice and let it slide slowly back down. The other knife needed an extra tug it's sharp point sticking into the wood. Matt ran his fingers along the blade, it was finely sharp, long and narrow, he had no idea what type of knife it was but it looked perfect. The wooden handle also felt reassuring in his hand, more like a weapon than a kitchen instrument. A door slammed upstairs and then the creaking of the staircase as the well built man came down to the hallway.

Matt leant against the kitchen sink, the knife held behind him running along the back of his leg.

"Come through, I will get us a drink." He turned and entered the other door leading from the hallway. Matt followed, the smile on his face never changing, his facial muscles beginning to ache.

The fella was now wearing a faded red surf t-shirt tucked into a pair of soft grey tracksuit bottoms. His back was turned as he poured what was presumably whiskey, from a decanter into two tumblers. The drink and glasses had been set on a tray with a gilded edge, it struck Matt as being horribly old fashioned but then he guessed the owners always put a few unwanted, odd items in rentals. Even with the vertical office style blinds open, the room was beginning to get dark, the black leather sofa and armchair a heavy sombre presence in the small space. The German turned round, one hand outstretched offering the glass to Matt.

"You do drink whiskey?"

"Yes" Matt wondered what sign he was waiting for.

"Here we are then."

And Matt accepted the glass with his left, his right hand appearing to be resting on his lower back.

"To us. New friends and maybe something more hmm?" And the tall blonde head began to move slowly towards Matthew's face, the ever smiling mouth now full lips together and the blue eyes beginning to close. Matt's stomach juices overturned, the simmering small fizz now rolling into large boiling rage and as the face grew just three inches from his he brought the knife round, manoeuvring the point upwards. It's smooth flow through the air stopped as it reached the firm stomach of the leering man in front of him. His arm muscles tensed as he forced it into his torso. Puncturing the flesh it then moved quickly again as it passed through the soft organs inside. Matt then angled it upwards again and thrust it into the gasping man's chest cavity. The eyes had opened wide with fear and then confusion before the pain reached his mind. As the knife penetrated his lungs a rasp of air escaped from his throat before being smothered by the sound of liquid. A deep moan began to rise from inside the crumpling man, his glass falling to the floor he grabbed Matt's shoulders with his two strong hands, clutching at the fabric of his sweatshirt. He began to slide downwards but Matt kept the force down his arm, the knife fighting to go deeper against the falling man's body. Warm blood flooded his hand and poured down his arm, he could hear the sound of it's soft plopping as it soaked into the pale blue carpet underneath them. His arm was beginning to shake with the exertion of holding the weight of this athletic man on the knife and he wiggled it out of the soft, splitting cavity allowing the body to fall on the floor. On all fours now, the wretched man was still gasping for air. Matt stood back, breaking the contact the dying man's hands had on his shoes. He watched the blood spreading into the carpet as it began to pour from his nose and wondered if he needed to do anything more. Taking a step to the side he bent down to try and get a better idea of what was going on underneath the man's body. Still on all fours there was a gap between his belly and the crimson floor. With a slurping noise, the man's grey intestines began to slither from the wound in his gut, slipping on top of one another into a wet, slimy mound on the floor.

It was now too disgusting for him to watch and so, leaving the poor creature lying in his own entrails, Matt walked into the kitchen.

Shit, he was a mess. There was blood everywhere, his clothes were covered and he had brought a trail of it into the kitchen. He stripped naked and threw everything, including his sneakers into the sink. He would have to use the faggot's shower and get some clean gear on. He stuck his head out of the kitchen doorway and around the edge of the lounge, the guy was slumped on the ground, his back to him, and thankfully, that dreadful gasping and gurgling had stopped. He giant strided past the lounge door, not wanting to reveal his nakedness to the poof, and lightly ran up the staircase. At the top of the stairs was the door to the bathroom, Matt elbowed it open with his left arm and stretched over the bathroom mat to stand in the bath. The shower was attached to the wall and a clear plastic curtain ran on hooks along the perimeter. As he watched the pink coloured water spinning down the plughole he tried to formulate a plan. He didn't want to leave the body here, the sooner someone discovered the geezer was dead the sooner his spending was over. He needed to get rid of it somehow but how the hell was he going to move a whole body out of the place without anyone noticing, he didn't have a car so stuffing him into a boot was no option. Leaning through the shower curtain he picked up a wooden nailbrush from the sinks soap dish. The bristles were well worn, like a toothbrush that had seen better days. Scratching the blood from under his nails it suddenly occurred to him that he was wasting his time. There was no point cleaning himself like this now, he needed to chop the body up and then he could get it out of here in bits.

His knees sank into the foul smelling carpet. Full of every kind of bodily fluid imaginable it squelched each time he moved, soaking through his jeans his legs began to feel wet and sticky. Lifting the dead weight of the head and the leg furthest away from him he heaved the body over onto it's back. With a sucking noise the stomach and intestines fell out leaving the torso flabby and soft. Picking up the bread knife he began to saw it through the flesh of the man's neck, the skin moved annoyingly underneath the blade before he managed to stab in the sharp end and then widen the gash with the serrated edge of the knife. The skin flapped apart revealing the black red depths, more blood oozed from the opening, Matt's hands were completely smothered and he struggled to maintain his grip on the handle of the knife. With large sweeping motions he managed to cut through the muscle, he was already beginning to sweat with exertion and the enormity of the task started to overwhelm him. Gritting his teeth he continued sawing until the knife struck the bone. He stood on his knees, pulling the head into him. Holding it with both hands he twisted it as far to the right as his straining muscles would allow. With a sharp crack the head suddenly moved easily and with more leverage left and right, it crunched apart and the heavy body slid slowly down Matt's legs, blood streaming from the open neck. Dropping the head onto the black bin bag beside him, he began to laugh quietly to himself, the relief of this first accomplishment, without thinking he brushed the back of his hand across his forehead smearing blood across his face. He looked down at the blank face, the cold blue eyes were staring straight towards him, the hair was stuck down with clots of blood, dried streams ran from the nostrils into the ear cavities. He turned the rubbish bag inside out, enclosing it, he didn't want that fucker watching him as he started on the rest of the body.

The contents of the last bag had been the worst; the organs that had slipped out from the gash in the man's stomach. With no gloves he had to scoop the quivering, floppy entrails in his hands, like a string of purple, grey sausages, he struggled to gain a grip. He began to feel lightheaded and the warm, wet mess in his arms seemed further and further from him, a cold sweat rose on his forehead and saliva began to stream into his mouth. He fought to gain control, he didn't want to leave his own vomit in this as well. He swallowed repeatedly, imagining that the shapeless flesh was nothing to do with a human body, screwing his nostrils shut and keeping his face turned away from the foul bag.

It was around two in the morning by the time he had finished, five bin bags were sat on the kitchen floor, even though he had tried to tie them tightly the smell still pervaded, it seemed to coat the inside of his nostrils. On top of the pile of body parts was the carpet. There was no way he could clean it and he didn't want to leave the awful mess, if the landlords stuck their heads in then they would be pissed off about the lack of carpet but there was no reason to think the bloke was dead. Even the ceiling had needed to be washed, to get through the larger bones he'd needed to hammer the kitchen knife, the blood splattering up the walls. After a hot shower that left his tired muscles trembling, he sat back in the bleach smelling lounge. Leaning on the coffee table the passport, drivers license and credit cards of the broken man in front of him, he started laughing again. His voice sounded crazy in the quiet house and he thought of the dead man bagged in the kitchen. It'd be alright, the bloke was a faggot anyway. First thing in the morning he was heading into town for a bit of shopping, he loved shopping, it's what mattered nowadays;

without the latest gear you were nobody. He would hire a car with this blokes id and then run to the local tip to dump the body, if he did it quickly then the smell shouldn't be too bad and by the time it was, everyone else's rubbish would be on top of it anyway. While he had the car he would drop in a present for mum before he left the country, she could do with a new video recorder. A present from her son would make her smile. With a plan in place his mind felt at rest and a yawn developed, in the house alone he let it stretch his face completely open, enjoying the large aw that escaped. He needed sleep otherwise he'd just fuck up tomorrow. He'd sleep in the bed upstairs and then strip it and dump the linen in the morning too.

"What are you doing here?" June was peed off. She thought he'd left the country.

"Got a present for you mum." Looking at the cardboard box in Matt's arms, interest and greed began to smooth out the cross lines across her face. "Aren't you going to let me in then?"

June stepped away from the door. "You'll have to come and talk to me in the kitchen, I'm busy."

The deep fat fryer sizzled as she pulled out the wire cage, fat golden chips glistened in the basket. "You hungry?"

"Yes please mum. Have you seen what I got you?"

He'd placed the box on the kitchen table, a diagram of the video machine on the outside.

"Yeah, you got me a new video player. I've only just got used to working the last one."

"This one's easier, they made them really simple to understand now."

Eggs splattered and spat from the frying pan, June stood back slightly, avoiding the burning oil spitting into her face. She tipped the chips onto kitchen roll, the fat spreading through the white paper.

"Get the knives and forks and we'll eat in the lounge." Matt dutifully stood up and set each plate, with knife and fork onto a tray. His stomach growled and he could almost smell his own hungry breath. "I'm starving mum."

"Good."

They sat in the lounge in complete silence, each of them in an armchair concentrating on every mouthful. The only sounds were that of their food squelching between their teeth and the sharply ticking clock on the mantelpiece. The atmosphere was sharply cracked by the shrill ringing of the doorbell, whoever was outside keeping their finger on the buzzer.

"Bloody hell." June put her tray on the floor and heaved herself from the chair. Matt craned his neck round to peer through the net curtains and try to gain a glimpse of the visitor.

He sat still, holding his knife and fork in the air as he strained to hear the conversation in the hallway. The lounge door opened and a young male police officer entered the room, Matt noticed the well defined forearms exposed from the short sleeve shirt, following him was a tall, female officer, her cuffs already in her hands.

"Hello Matthew, you were supposed to be back in the prison yesterday."

"Oh was it yesterday? I thought I had another day, I must have lost track."

"Well come on, we'll get you back there and they can deal with it."

His mother stayed in the hallway, as he was led past her she turned her eyes downwards to the floor.

-12-

Guy

Guy had never been to Cancun but looking at the postcard, it seemed to live up to his expectations. The white sand was speckled with brown dots, small splashes of colour breaking up the homogenous fleshy swarm, hundreds of bodies in colourful bikinis. Against the softness of the sand and the curling waves of ocean, stark, straight hotels rose against the beach, hard lines standing fast against nature's playground.

It must have been the third or fourth postcard so far. Guy enjoyed receiving the small square windows of life around the world, the pictures seemed unreal in the grey setting of prison life in England. Cloudless blue skies, turquoise oceans, white smiles in mocha faces, unattainable beauty. Flipping the cards over Badger would then struggle to convey a message to him. His written language was so appalling Guy found himself chuckling at the almost ludicrous mistakes yet there was always one phrase the same, a line that Badger had proudly learnt to spell correctly, 'Wish you were here?' and then the little smiley face. The sentiment was always upbeat, business was going well, life was turning around, the darkness did not soak into these little snapshots, maybe it didn't exist in Badger's outside world or maybe he was just concealing it. Guy dropped the postcard into the wire bin of the tv lounge before heading out to the tennis courts. He had plenty of time to spare so chose to walk through the prison garden on the way. Grass verges ran alongside the gravelled pathways and the first spring daffs were bobbing their yellow heads in the cold breeze. Buds had begun to form on the trees whose bare branches spiked the air, sharply black against the low, white sky. Several inmates were working in the vegetable garden, a spade striking the hard earth in a thumping, scratching rhythm, the man working it shirtless in the cool air. Another bloke worked alongside him, forking over the sliced clods of earth in an attempt to soften the bed ready for planting. Guy felt a gentle warmth on his hair and raised his face to catch the brief appearance of watery sun that streamed through a break in the clouds. He could feel the dark shadows under his eyes tingling in the heat, the colour slowly rising in his cheeks. Gratitude left a comfortable smile resting on his face, it occurred to him that he must be totally institutionalised, for at that moment, he wished for nothing more in life. It seemed a blackbird agreed with him, it's spring song rising up and down, like melodious bubbles bursting from it's throat.

Two tennis courts were enclosed by a six foot high mesh fence. One court was already in use, the popping of the tennis ball being thwacked across the net cut through the crisp air. Leaning against the fence Guy recognised the short, stocky figure of his cellmate, on noticing Guy he raised an arm and hollered across *"Ahoy there Captain!."* Guy laughed and raised his racket in response. He picked up his pace to join his exuberant friend. Lesley Gates had been a breath of fresh air, a strong, pot bellied forty year old American. Okay he was loud and coarse and maybe he was over opinionated, opinions that would never stand up to intelligent scrutiny but, after all, this was a prison and anyone with a brain, common sense and self control would never end up here. For all that, Lesley was a true comrade, he'd throw his arm around you, laugh from the pit of his belly and draw in anyone that needed to feel included. He was determined to make money, enough money to buy glittery watches, baby Bentley's and a gated house on a private estate in the home counties. Unfortunately for Lesley, his excesses drew unwelcome attention and no sooner had he cracked it, he ended up serving another lump of time.

Guy rose his voice above the breeze. "Hey buddy, you up for a severe thrashing?"

Lesley roared with laughter, like an ageing lion his wavy blonde hair ran in thin lines across the top of his head, curls bunched around his ears. "No way Guy my friend, are you ready?"

The two men walked on to the tarmac court and after much wrangling eventually flipped a coin to determine who was going to start with the slanting morning sun in their face.

Guy hoped that his childhood tennis lessons would give him the skill required to beat the ox of a man waiting at the other end but as the ball skimmed the net and flew towards him in a yellow fuzzy blur he realised he was also going to need to call upon every ounce of strength to return the ball in a similarly powerful fashion. For an hour and a half the highly competitive American was silent with determination until finally, red faced and sweating like a horse he claimed a slim victory. As he walked to the net he pulled the white polo shirt away from his body, flapping the front to send cool waves of air over his stomach. Guy raised his blistered hand to shake the strong hard one proffered over the net. Just as their fingers were about to touch, Lesley withdrew his hand raising a thumb to his nose and waggling his fingers whilst a thick lipped raspberry spluttered towards Guy's face.

"Told you I'd beat you, you pommy bastard." Turning to walk sideways along the net Guy then felt himself propelled forward as a large hand slapped him in the middle of his back. "Better luck next time, it was a good game though eh?"

"A blinder mate."

Standing in the shower block, Guy raised his face to the fine needle spray, feeling his muscles relax and his tired head awaken. As he closed his eyes and mouth to the soap streaming from his hair, his ears were assaulted by the deep, echoing voice of Lesley singing Neil Diamond.

"Hey Captain, when you get out of here are you going to meet up with your mate that keeps sending the postcards?"

Guy let the water run across his eyes clearing his face of soap before turning round, concentrating the jet of water between his shoulder blades.

"Not if I can help it, the bloke was a bit of a nut."

"He must be doing all right for himself though, he's travelling all over the place looking at those cards."

"Yeah, I know, nothing I'd be interested in though."

"What about me? Is it worth an introduction?"

Guy laughed and raised his head to look at the man standing two nozzles down from him. His hair was plastered onto his head in a dark slick, the thick dark eyelashes gave him an almost forlorn look. "Not unless you're interested in the meat trade. He was working in the butchery before he left."

Lesley squeezed a large dollop of clear gel into his right palm and, closing his eyes, worked it into a furious stream of bubbles on his head. "Nah, can't say that sounds very inspiring. Hey, did I tell you I can get an American newspaper here? I've put it on my order, a little news from the home country."

"I didn't think it was cool to be American anymore"

A sponge, heavy and sodden smacked Guy in the face.

"Watch yourself mate, us Yanks still have our pride."

-13-

Matthew

The tip of his nose touched the cool window of the plane, his chin sitting hard in his palm, the nobble of his elbow resting on the sill. Approaching Mexico City, warm familiarity soaked into the sharp edges of Matt's consciousness. The pink and red roofs of the suburbs stretched below him like a patchwork quilt, the streets running in orderly squares until the major highways began to dissect the grid, cutting through in diagonal lines so long that they seemed to disappear into the horizon. The small square houses began to break up into industrial plots and tall, concrete buildings a mix of old colonial and sky reaching commercial offices. Green stretches of park, huge trees that, from Matt's birds eye perspective, looked like soft, dark mossy growths, the luscious cool spaces vibrant against the sand coloured desertscape. Through the haze of pollution and hot, wilting air, the mountains curved gently around the sweeping, spreading city, gently cradling it's enormous human population, the blue sky thinning to white next to the purple peaks.

He had made it. Finally, after another stretch in prison, paying an extortionate amount of money for an inmates id and risking Heathrow airport, he was going to join his family. It was plain sailing now, the rest of his life was in front of him. He would never have to return to the grey country that despised him, that had always rejected him, never understood him, from now on he would command respect and be the controller of his destiny. He had gained strength from his book, there was someone out there who understood him and had helped teach him the way forward. He'd killed before, that German bloke, and he'd got away with it. Now he was trained, he would be professional about it. The hero in his book wasn't as well travelled as Matthew, that was where he had an advantage; no need to shit on his own doorstep.

The ping of the seatbelt sign turned his gaze from the window back to the cabin. He clicked his belt closed and shut his eyes concentrating on the familiar landing sensations; the air escaping from his ears, the gentle lurching in his stomach as the plane descended, the nasal female voice rattling English and Spanish information through the PA system, her commentary competing against the scream of the engines preparing to land. As the plane bumped, heaved into the air then bumped again onto the hard tarmac, Matthew opened his eyes, renewed life and determination glittering in the dark irises.

She could feel the crumbs of bread and the soft dust of flour sticking to the soles of her feet as she moved around the small, cramped kitchen. The smell of fried onions and diesel sat on the gentle breeze through the open shutters, raised voices from the apartment below and the ups and downs of children screaming as they chased one another around the rusting climbing frame of the communal playground. Philly was sitting at the little kitchen table, the unconscious twitching of her foot causing the wooden chair to rock on the uneven surface of the floor. In a monotone voice she read from her school library book as Nieve cooked their tea. Over the din of the frying pan Nieve became aware that her daughter had stopped speaking.

"Carry on honey."

The little girl looked at her, two deep brown eyes slightly accusing, Nieve knew she had been caught out, Philly was not one to be fooled.

"You weren't listening mum."

"Yes I was, the little boy was supposed to sell the donkey"

Philly looked back down to her book and continued her slow Mexican drawl. Nieve added a wrinkly pepper to the rice sizzling in the wok and then turned her attention to the fridge, scanning the white shelves for a forgotten piece of salami or something similarly long in life span. Disappointed by the absence of a surprise tasty morsel she opened the pantry door and reached for a tin of beans. The buzz of the intercom was more like a sudden electrical spark and called out it's high pitched alert to no avail. It reached Philly's ears on it's second attempt.

"Mum, someone's at the door."

Nieve turned from the kitchen top, frowning at the door across the lounge space. She had just achieved penetration with the can opener and was reluctant to put it down unfinished.

"Oh who can that be?"

"Shall I get it mum?" Nieve resigned herself to putting the can on the top with the opener still attached. "No, I'll get it." Wiping her hands on the tea towel hanging from the oven rail, she crossed the lounge as the buzzer bleated for a third time. As she placed her hand on the door latch she leant her head to the spy hole for a casual peek. The distorted, gold fish image made her heart stop and her eye strained to get closer, her eyelashes brushing the metal surround. Slowly twisting the latch she breathed in.

"Hello Nieve." His smile was the same, reminiscent of a Cheshire cat, but the eyes didn't belong with it, they reminded her more of the glazed expression on the large dead fish at the market. Maybe it was too much time in the prisons, maybe his soul needed nurturing.

"Hello Matty. What are you doing here?"

"I thought you needed me Nieve. I'm here to look after you and my little girl."

At the thought of her daughter Nieve felt a sharp pain slice through her heart.

"Philly, her name is Philly."

"Beautiful, can I come in?"

"Yes but, Matty?"

"What?"

"I don't know that it is good for you live here. I not sure it best. My husband, you know the policeman, is Philly's dad, I don't want for her to be upset or um how do you say, mixed?"

"Confused. I know, I'm not here for that. I want to get to know her better, then, maybe, I could tell her the truth. I just want to look after you both. I've got a place closer to town, it's going to be good Nieve, I've got plans, we're going to be good again."

"Hmm, I think you come in." Nieve was conscious of sounds along the corridor, the apartment block was a small, tongue wagging community and she wasn't even sure herself yet how she was going to handle this situation.

The smell of spicy food pulled Matt's senses into the small space of the kitchen ahead. Pots and pans were stacked onto an open shelving rack, mismatched china; orange, yellow and blue, plates and bowls were pushed onto a shelf over the sink, not quite deep enough for the plate's circumference. The sink sat into a stainless steel worktop, the taps tall and slightly brassy with age, a bright yellow jay cloth was slung over in a feeble attempt at airing. The floor was bare chipboard, stained to resemble wood, the twisted patchwork fabric of the durry mats providing some softness under foot.

And then he noticed her. Underneath the open shutters, sitting at a wooden table, big enough for just two chairs, sat a little girl in school uniform. Her dark hair was pulled back into a ponytail that rested black against her white, short sleeved shirt. Caramel legs stuck out from a navy blue skirt, her bare feet swinging under the table. Matthew was no good with children's ages but guessed she must have been around six, her little face was still round with puppy fat and her inquisitive brown eyes were wide with unashamed curiosity.

"Philly, this is Matthew, he is an old friend of mummy's, you may remember mummy talking about him before." Philly nodded unconvincingly.

"Aren't you going to say hello?"

"Hola."

Matt smiled, could this exotic, pretty little thing really be his? He looked to Nieve, she was thinner, her eyes harder and the creases on her face more permanent but she was still lovely and he knew, he just knew that this child was his. Nieve could only have borne a baby to him, only their love could have created a child, the whole thing with that officer was a mistake, she was just scared of being on her own that was all.

Matt listened intently as Nieve and Philly communicated to one another in Spanish, he could understand the odd word and knew his wife well enough to read her tone. The little girl stood up and began to sweep her school books into the pink rucksack that had been shoved underneath her chair. Nieve was busy stirring the contents of a cast iron black pan.

"Can you bring the chair Matty?"

Matt looked round the living space and presumed she must mean a rocking chair that was pushed into the corner. He tipped off a skinny ginger cat that had curled itself into a neverending circle and picked up the cushion that had fallen off with it. Covered in white and ginger hair he turned it upside down and lifted the chair up to the table. Philly was setting out fabric dinner mats and carefully placing a fork on each. Matt smiled at her, she tried to return it but the corners of her mouth puckered with shyness and she cast her eyes down to the table, straightening the forks.

"Are you very hungry?" Nieve looked at the large man taking up so much space in her little home and worried at how far she could make the contents of the pan stretch.

"Mmmm starving."

Inspiration dropped a pebble into her thoughts and she opened the bread tin. Whacking the oven up to full, she threw in the day old bread to warm and added a wooden chopping board and knife to the table.

As they ate, Nieve found herself stealing little glances at Matty. There was something reassuring about having a male presence at the table again and it was so nice to have another adult to cook for. Sometimes, with just a child to appreciate your hard work, it just didn't seem worth it and there were days when food was a necessity and not a pleasure. She had also learnt to constantly live with a minor panic contained in her sub consciousness like a demented animal kept in a cage. There was a constant fear that she would let a ball drop somewhere and her daughter would be affected. She knew she could always rely on something being sent from England but he was so far away and as more time passed between visits, how much longer would he keep it up? She watched as Matty and Phil tried to talk to one another, pointing at things, acting out questions and answers, the little girl laughing at the silly adult and wondered if maybe this old love of hers was worth another chance.

His place was certainly a lot nicer than where she lived. Four steps ran up to two front doors, one was dark green, the colour of ferns deep in the forest, the paint was blistered in the heat and strips were flaking off, exposing the light wood underneath. The door on the right hand side was brick red, so newly painted a smudge of paint on the top step exposed the decorator's incompetence. The house was narrow, a line of terraces jostling for space in the city, but it was proud, for however modest, it was a house and did not have anyone living above or below it. Terracotta roof tiles rippled out from the top floor, creating a precious line of shade over the front porch. She followed him into the red house, their shoes clacking loudly on the wooden floor, a faint echo as the sparsely furnished home failed to cushion any noise. The space was cool, the thick stone walls protecting the occupants from the heat outside. Philly squeezed past her mother and tugged at Matt's arm.

"Si?" He looked down at the excited face. She babbled back to him in Spanish and pointed at the staircase. Matt looked over her head to Nieve's laughing face. "She wants to choose her bedroom."

Matt laughed "Oh, of course." And taking her cue, Philly bounced up the stairs, the banister shaking as the old boards creaked. A thought struck Matt and the laugh quickly fell "What if she chooses our room? There are only two bedrooms."

"No worry, little girls like bedrooms pequeno."

Matt stepped closer to Nieve, sliding his arms around her waist and clasping them in the small of her back. Pulling her into him, his groin pressed hard into her.

"We need to christen every room."

She leaned backwards "It's so hot Matty." His arms dropped like stones, suspended limply from the broad shoulders. A sneer crawled underneath his skin as the laughter fell from his face. Walking into the lounge he called over his shoulder "I guess you'll be wanting to make changes, you know, the female touch."

She stepped into the living room, running the width of the house, it was small but had the bonus of being situated at the rear of the property, two glass doors opened onto a paved courtyard, a fig tree dominated the shady space, the air around it vibrating with the songs of the fat bodied cicadas. A pot bellied chimnea hid in the darkest corner, green lichen crept up the orange terracotta and Nieve knew that, were she to move it, a group of shiny, brown cockroaches would scuttle away from underneath it to hide in the cracked walls.

She stepped quietly up behind Matt, touching the loose fabric at the back of his cotton shirt "How can you pay for this Matty?"

His head whipped round, and she felt pinned underneath his force "I can pay for this, don't ever question me, I will provide for you"

Her hands rose instinctively, her palms towards him like a shield "I not question you Matty, I just don't want the police and prisons, you know there is Philly to take care for."

The light footsteps trickled down the staircase, Matt looked up to the small figure standing at the door, he smiled and straightened his back away from her mother. "No-one is going without." Not understanding, but feeling the tension break, Philly entered the room, tugging her mother's hand and babbling away. Nieve laughed and allowed herself to be pulled up the staircase to the little girl's chosen room.

Matt stepped into the courtyard, behind the chirruping of the small critters inhabiting the parched shrubbery, the constant murmur of the city tugged at his senses, reminding him of a faster lane that needed to be jumped on.

The hum of morning traffic increased in synch with the light filtering through the half open shutters. The rising sun washed the sky watercolour pink, blending the white mosquito net with the new cotton sheets, Nieve felt her mind gently swaying between the lightly fingered hold of her last dream and the soft, muted light of her bedroom. He was away and Philly was still asleep; bringing her arms up behind her head and enjoying the time between waking and having to raise herself from her comfortable, personal space. She was beginning to manage the nagging voice of misgiving, leaning to squash it down, distracting herself with shopping for her new home, enjoying the small luxuries like the beautiful new sheets that rested against her naked skin. It was easier to ignore Matt's failings when there was plenty of money coming into the house. He had rented a small shop and stocked it with American t-shirts, sourcing the clothes had become a regular excuse for him to travel, taking off for a few days at a time. Sadness flickered in her chest as she recalled Matt's twisted face the day before. His features were contorted by the dark element in him that rose against her, fighting any form of control that she tried to assert. She knew he loved her, she had never known anyone to be so totally devoted to her but he couldn't handle any hint of criticism. She had only wanted to press him a little, his income was so erratic that she couldn't help but worry that he had returned to his old ways. She hadn't wanted to accuse him, she'd only wanted reassurance. He had stood in the hallway, his hand resting on the pulley handle of his small case. His hair was neatly combed away from his face, his pale pink shirt immaculately pressed, polished brown brogues peeped out from under his moleskin trousers. He looked so respectable, so handsome that a small butterfly of pride spread it's wings inside her chest but, as she studied his face, straightening his collar in the hallway mirror, it shrank with a fine tremor of fear. There was something in him she couldn't reach.

"Matty, what are you doing when you're away?"

He continued to look into the mirror. "Working of course."

"I know, working, but I still worry about what working."

His eyes slid to catch hers, looking at her through the glass. "What are you trying to say?"

The words sliced out from the side of his mouth, Nieve felt her resolve weaken "Nothing, nothing Matty, I'm sorry."

"I'll see you in a couple of days." And without a kiss, a touch, a moment's tenderness, he opened the front door, the heat ballooning into the cool hallway, and walked to the taxi parked on the road out front. She leant on the door frame and watched the lime green cab move away from her until it disappeared at the end of the road.

Dirty Luggage

He was a citizen of the world. His case rattled along the polished floor of the airport as he strode along the check out counters looking for his airline. He loved Nieve, everything he did was for her but why did it feel so good to get away? When he was travelling he felt like someone, someone interesting, did people wonder where he was going, what his business was? Somehow, constantly moving landscapes, city's and airports surrounded by strangers, it all felt like his territory. With the anonymity that his movement gave him, he felt in control.

He approached the smiling girl on the check in desk, her eyes like hard boiled eggs rimmed by black liner, her lips like a slice of bright red tomato. Handing across his passport and ticket, she gave no more than a cursory glance at the photo, he knew he looked far too respectable to be travelling on a false identity, why would he? After all he looked just like any other international businessman and he wasn't travelling far, a few hours just to a neighbouring country. Four days working and then back home, his usual pattern.

Comfortably ensconced in the plane, his luggage stored in the overhead locker and a small glass of red wine on his lap tray, he opened his favourite novel. It was a paperback and the front cover was now beginning to look tired. The glossy black picture was creased, fine white lines breaking the drama of the illustrated weapon. It was a shame, he didn't feel it did the book justice to look so inconsequential. Resting his head on the chair he relished the opening lines, anticipating the journey the character was going to take him on.

After three hours the plane began landing preparations. Matt closed his book and placed it on his lap, staring blankly through the mist on the window, the clouds an ethereal blanket smothering the Airbus. Fine threads pulled him close to the character in the novel, like a brother he felt his presence in his soul. He allowed the cool, white anger of his hero to enlarge in his chest, capturing the emotion and harnessing his power as he collected his belongings and filed slowly off the plane.

-14-

Sandra, North America

Sandra Robertson felt a small surge of panic as she threw clothes into the open suitcase on her bed. She was sure she had thought of everything, organised by nature, every detail of the trip had been played in her head, every eventuality considered, down to sticking the telephone number of the vets on the fridge in case something happened to the cat. It was leaving the kids really, it was supposed to be them flying the nest and her sitting at home worrying, instead, she was the one pursuing educational ambitions and they were left at home, alone. She tried not to think about it. Lewes was twenty-two and Kitty nineteen. Old enough. Old enough for what? Could they handle an accident? Would they know what to do in a medical emergency, God forbid a terrorist attack? And even if none of that happened, what if they had a few friends over and the place got gate crashed? Sandra tried to get a hold, telling herself to calm down, she had always been there for them, more than some mothers and there had to come a time when they had to fend for themselves. It was just they were so close. After Derek died, the three of them had leant so heavily on each other, they were so strong she was proud of the team effort they had all made. It would be okay, they were good kids, sensible and she could trust them. She zipped the fabric case closed, straining to get the two ends to meet. Standing at the window she looked down to the front yard, smothered in a golden layer of brown and red autumnal leaves, it was the annual New Hampshire display of nature's beauty turning into mush on her front lawn. She must remember to ask Lewes to try and tidy it up while she was away.

She just had time to join the kids over breakfast before Kitty ran her to the airport. The solid wood staircase was polished to burnished copper and Sandra cursed her cleaning efficiency as she nearly broke her neck, slipping on the top step in her flight socks. Gripping the handrail she eyed Derek's photographs lining the wall, what he had felt were deeply artistic but actually, turned out to be incredibly conservative close up shots of summer flowers and autumnal leaves, a gentle touch to one or two corners and she was satisfied they were all straight. A golden shaft of morning light streamed through the stained glass in the front door, red and green orbs danced along the hallway, the dust sparkling in a shimmering duet. It was all so lovely, peaceful, she really didn't want to leave her home, yet the old Sandra, the frizzy haired anthropology student of eighteen, was beginning to speak to her again, a fiery, confidant girl who believed she was capable of anything, was telling her she still could, it wasn't over, there was a lot of life still to be lived. It was true, she knew it wouldn't be long before her family left her and what then? Rattling around this big old house on her own, trying to re-establish a social life just so she had a reason to get out of her dressing gown every morning? No. This way was better, she would have a profession, a label, a little self-respect.

Kitty was standing in the kitchen, juggling the toaster, the kettle and a pan of eggs. Lewes sat at the breakfast bar, his back to her, bent over an enormous cereal bowl slurping the wet contents into his mouth as quickly as possible.

Kitty threw her an enormous smile, the sun catching the top of her head, golden strands of hair seeming to float around her brunette mane.

"Morning mom, how you feeling?"

Sandra considered the intensity of the butterflies in her stomach. "Oh, okay I guess" she walked up to Lewes, resting her hand on one of his shoulders, she could feel the hard bumps and dips of his muscles, lean and taut with youth and athleticism. He placed his large hand on top of hers "Hey mom."

She kissed the top of his head before pulling out the stool next to him, Kitty pushed a mug of coffee across the bench to her.

"We'll be okay you know, you don't need to worry" Kitty caught her eye

"I know honey, I'm going to miss you though"

Lewes dug her in the ribs with his elbow, his spoon raised in it's perpetual circle from bowl to mouth. "Aw mom, don't be a sissy"

"This'll be good for you mom, you're going to really enjoy it. You'll be learning loads of cool stuff and you'll forget all about us."

Sandra looked at her daughter, how had she managed to create such beautiful children?

"Thanks Kit."

"Right, well, we better get a move on or you'll miss your flight."

Sandra cursed her decision to wear loafers. They seemed a comfortable, sensible choice back in the cold atmosphere of New Hampshire but, standing in the arrivals hall of Guatemala City airport, she could think of nothing else but opening her luggage and pulling out a pair of flip flops. Her cotton t-shirt felt like a blanket and even the backs of her knees were sweating in the humid, balmy, human infested airport. She scanned the information signs, happy that she could at least recognise most of the Spanish words. She didn't want the intrusion of a porter, preferring to make her own way to the taxi rank without the embarrassment of trying to find money for an unnecessary tip. If she continued in the direction of the exit, following the Salida signs, then surely the taxi rank would be comfortingly positioned directly outside. Putting on imaginary blinkers, avoiding the eyes and ignoring the offers of guidance from the locals, she trundled her suitcase towards the open entranceway.

"Are you looking for a taxi?" a very English voice attracted her attention. Unsure if it was meant for her, she looked casually to her right, not wanting to appear interested if it wasn't. A dark haired man was walking alongside her, wearing a pink cotton shirt and smart trousers he looked like a businessman. He was also white skinned, in his thirties and smiling at her.

"Sorry to bother you, I just thought maybe you'd like a little bit of help. You look a bit lost."

Sandra felt some of the tension leave her shoulders, it was such a relief to be looking at a welcoming, knowledgeable, white male face "Is it that obvious?" she laughed "I hoped I was fooling everyone!"

The man laughed in response, a warm sound that seemed to resonate deep in his chest which, she noticed, was just at her head height.

"Don't worry, you're probably fooling the locals. I know it can be a bit daunting when you're new to a strange city. Look, I know this place well, I regularly have to travel here for business, what hotel are you staying at? We could share a cab, it might just help you get there safely eh?"

Sandra thought it was a brilliant idea. She had two days to amuse herself and get her bearings before meeting with her tour. "That's a wonderful idea, if we're going in the same direction, I'm staying at the Hylux."

Pleasant surprise registered on the man's face "That's where I was planning to stay! Well, there you go, perfect."

They walked side by side to the exit, the warmth that had greeted them before now swelled into an all encompassing suffocating hold. Sandra felt her cheeks glowing as the blood raced to the skin's surface, desperately trying to cool down.

"Don't worry, you'll get used to it."

"Huh?"

"The heat, you'll get used to it. Hopefully the cab will be air conditioned. Simon, by the way." He smiled.

"Sandra." She returned his smile.

As he predicted, the taxi was like a tiny fridge on wheels, the cool leather penetrated the back of her t-shirt and she had to keep suctioning her legs from the seat, not wanting to leave any evidence of the sweat behind her knees. The young man gave instructions to the cab driver and they whistled away from the airport, the suspension of the well used vehicle wobbling slightly, sending the cross dangling from the rear view mirror into a perpetual swinging motion.

"You're American right?"

"Yes, first time to Guatemala." Sandra wondered whether she should have sounded less of a virgin traveller.

"What brings you here?"

"Oh, I'm an old anthropologist at heart. Veered right away from it when I had the children but now I've begun to re-ignite my studies. My college professor put me in touch with a friend of his who conducts tours over here, the Mayan civilisations have always fascinated me, and it just felt like the right time to take a trip."

"Absolutely, I'm sure you're gonna love it here. Just be a little on your guard, I couldn't help noticing how you carry your handbag over your shoulder. Never a good way to carry anything valuable, wherever you are."

Sandra felt a little patronised and naïve. "Yes, a silly mistake, I must remember to shake old habits."

She turned her attention to the city streaming past her window. Certain aspects looked European to her American eyes, the wide avenues lined with mature trees, the soft stone of colonial architecture. Interspersed with the older city, cranes towered over large sections, evidence of new prosperity as sharp edged, blank concrete buildings rose in competition with one another. Amongst the cabs and smart city commuter cars, open top trucks piled high with provisions; chickens, blankets and family members, chugged alongside the downtown traffic, puffing dark clouds of diesel into the hot city. The sidewalks were peppered with weathered brown faces, country people trying to conduct a little business in the city, Sandra couldn't guess their ages, they were either the same as her but with skin creased from squinting against the sun all their lives or they were sprightly and sinewy older folk, kept strong by their labours.

The click clacking of the cab's indicator drew Sandra's attention into more focus, straightening her back she craned to try and catch an early glimpse of their hotel.

"Here we are." The young man released his seatbelt as the cab curved into the drop off zone of a bland, westernised hotel. The national and hotel chain flags tinkled on poles in the middle of the roundabout, advertising the homogenous rooms and level of service to be expected in every country. Sandra felt the rush of embarrassment as they drew closer to the point where the fare would have to be paid, pulling her handbag onto her lap she found her purse and held it ostentatiously in one hand.

"I'll get this, you've been so kind."

"Oh no, it's the least I can do, I was coming here anyway."

Sandra wasn't sure how far to take the argument before it became awkward. "Please, at least let me go halves."

"I'll tell you what, I'll get this and you can owe me a drink in the hotel bar."

Sandra felt her heart stop with a hard thump in her chest. Oh god, had she got this totally wrong? Was she so bad at reading men nowadays? Was this all just one big come on? Determined to keep her expression relaxed and neutral, she held his eyes whilst analysing his proposal. He was at least ten years younger than her, he was smart and obviously well travelled, she had detected a certain roughness in the tone of his voice but he was attractive and confident. He couldn't be interested in her surely? Her lips were just beginning to part, ready to try and form some kind of answer when he jumped in.

"I'm going to unpack, wash up and give wifey a call, she hates it when I'm away, then it might be quite nice to have a drink before I have to think about business tomorrow."

Relief, warm apologetic relief turned the corners of Sandra's mouth upwards. "Okay, sounds like a good plan, I can pick your brains about where I should spend my free day."

Sandra had booked a room at the front of the hotel, having come from the peace of the suburbs she wanted to enjoy the contrast of a city centre. She was also hoping that to absorb some of the local culture just by people watching from the distance of her hotel balcony. The natural light was beginning to lose intensity as the setting sun began to dip into the horizon, low enough now to be concealed by the city's structures, the soft golden light that lit the underside of the stationary clouds the only evidence that it had not disappeared completely. Sandra found the half light straining on her eyes, shadows becoming indistinct from their solid companions allowing her sight to relax, taking second place behind her hearing for sensation. The evening was layered with sound. The rumble and growl of the traffic was dominant but a pleasant symphony was created with the evening birdsong and the chorus of crickets that chirruped invisibly from the trees and grass verges surrounding the hotel. Sitting on the patio chair tiredness slowly crept into the corners of her mind. Her eyes stung underneath the heavy weight of her eyelids, drifting inside herself, small white spots flickered inside the closed shutters of her eyes, a gentle pull to dive deeper into the black comfort of sleep.

She jolted awake, her neck killing her as she straightened it from her chest. A loud knocking on the door jarred her senses, she wasn't sure how long she'd been asleep but the city had become an exotic night creature, cars turning into orange eyed creatures and unattractive buildings twinkling with white and neon lights. An army of ants filed in a solid black line to and from the empty complimentary biscuit packet she had left on the table and a mild prickling sensation around her ankles warned her of terrible itching to come from mosquito bites. She pushed herself up from the chair, her bottom stiff from the unforgiving plastic seat. Of course, it would be Simon. She paused briefly as she walked in front of the mirror, pushing the pins firmly back into the pleat at the back of her head and then walked up to the door.

"Hello, who is it?"

"Hi Sandra, it's me, Simon."

"Hang on just a minute while I unlock." And she began to run through the many bolts on the heavy, solid door. It all seemed a bit extreme but feeling they must be for good reason she had worried herself into locking every one. First she had to slide the bolt at the top and then, bending down, slide the matching one at the bottom. Then a long, black iron bolt that ran along the centre needed to be turned with a small paddle before opening. A twist of the latch opened the door which now hung open a few inches until, closing it again, she unhooked the gold chain. As she glimpsed Simon's face she laughed, "Sorry, just wanted to take precautions."

Simon laughed and took a step forward, entering the room. Sandra turned her back as she was about to say "I just need to sort myself out" but as the sentence formed in her mind a black fist smashed inside her brain, the words seeming to drop onto her bottom lip at the same time as losing any sense of having legs, as if they had just vanished. Her mind was a scrambled circuit of loose connections inside a husk that seemed to belong to nothing. Just as the sage green carpet came careering up to her face everything went dark.

Sitting on the toilet lid he found himself drifting into a trance like state as he stared at the bright crimson streak on the glossy white floor tiles. Luckily they were not porous so cleaning them shouldn't be a problem. The old lady was in the bath tub so she wasn't going anywhere and he could take five minutes to let his pulse rate settle. Rubbing his hands up and down his face, he tried to wake himself up, his eyes felt lead rimmed, the sides of his nose aching with a hollowness in the space his sunglasses had sat on all day. Pressing hard into his temples he hoped the bruising sensation would alleviate his brain's preoccupation with building a filthy headache. Standing at the sink he gazed at himself in the mirror. He'd started the day feeling fresh and young, a good shave, a little sunshine on his skin had left him buoyant but, now with a five o clock shadow and the garish white light of the bathroom, he looked grey and tired. Looking into the dark pools of his eyes he wondered who he was nowadays. There was a shaft of happiness, like sunlight falling on one side of his body; a beautiful woman, a daughter and his hunger for success was being fed, he knew how to make money and get away with it. Yet, underneath the warm layer of skin he still felt empty, well, not quite empty, sometimes, if he concentrated hard enough, he could feel deep swirls, like the dark, filthy water in the bottom of a barrel stirred with a stick. He was smart enough to know that maybe he should be trying to stop the swirl and examine it, yet it was like a piece of volcanic rock that weighted him down, a heavy presence in his mind that had always been there and he had tried to get rid of it in the past but nothing had worked. He'd tried to distract it, ignore it, throw it out of himself and towards other people but, at the most, it would cloud over for a little while before a moment's pause would feel it again, sitting there quietly, just waiting to be acknowledged. Nowadays he just accepted that it was a part of him. It made him special, unlike all the others, it was his secret, his power and superiority. Glancing down at the bath he remembered he had a lot of work to do, he wanted to get on with this one, she'd be missed pretty quickly.

Her clothes were in a pile on the floor, the sticky hammer slung on top. He pulled a roll of bin bags from his holdall and started ripping the bags along the perforations, flapping each one open, almost filling the small space with the floating plastic. Then he brought out his knives. Holding his favourite in one hand he gently ran his finger along the blade, his baby. He smiled to himself, it was so good to feel proud of something. He was a master, his blades were good enough to cut up a whole body without the constant distraction of sharpening. Laying it on the floor he rummaged in the bag for the solid piece of stone. A few swift strokes and the blade was ready.

Kneeling down, he leant over the bath, he had to rest his stomach against the edge offering his back some support. He held the top of the woman's head with his hand, his large fingers spreading through the fine, grey hair, his little finger sinking into the soft dip at the back where her skull had caved in when he bashed it. The blood around the wound was beginning to dry and felt sticky against the palm of his hand. Stretching her neck taut he pushed her head away from him, her slack jaw wobbling slightly, her tongue fell further down her throat causing a sound like mucous catching to break the silence in the room. It didn't worry him, there was no sound he hadn't heard before from a dead carcass. The knife sliced easily through her neck, reaching her cervical bones the movements became automatic as he dis-jointed the head from the body. He tipped the neck slightly towards the plug hole, the blood pouring out too quickly for the drain to keep up, a pool began to collect in the white tub. He stayed in the same position for several minutes, staring at the yellow grout in the tiles on the wall. He was so sick of dealing with blood that he had found this the quickest way to get rid of most of it before continuing to chop up the body. The flow slowed to a steady stream and he dropped the body down again, arching his back in a stomach splitting stretch before removing each limb from her torso.

The kettle rocked with the force of it's boiling and didn't seem to stop until Matthew flicked off the power at the plug socket. Pouring it into the mug the acrid smell of cheap coffee powder disappointed him, it wasn't going to hit the spot. Looking at the blood stain on the sage green carpet, he felt depressed. There was always so much fucking cleaning to do. The bathroom shone, five black bin bags neatly tied on the floor, but now he had to deal with the carpet. He should have dragged her into the bathroom before he hit her with the hammer. Sitting on the sofa he began to sift through her handbag while he waited for the coffee to cool. Two smiling faces leapt out from him as he opened her wallet. He'd forgotten she was a mum. Peering closer the son and daughter looked attractive and happy, he bet they were oh so fucking popular too, oh well, they looked like they were old enough to cope with losing a mother anyway. He was pleased to find a large quantity of currency and travellers cheques, that was always a quick, easy bonus. Everything he needed was there, her passport, bank account details and credit cards, he could change the passport easily enough, everything he needed was back in his hotel room. The thought made him check his watch, he'd better get a move on. Swallowing the coffee swiftly, still so hot it was almost scalding, he then turned his attention to the carpet. Using her clothes and a couple of hotel towels he managed to soak up and then spread the stain enough that no-one would notice it unless they were looking closely. It had taken a good half hour and now his insides were beginning to tickle with panic. He didn't want to stay in this room any longer, he kept looking at the door and the telephone beside the bed, imagining he'd heard a knock or the beginnings of a ring on the handset. He tipped the contents of her suitcase on to the bed, a professional looking camera fell out and bounced slightly off the mattress, landing on the floor with a thud. More travellers cheques were hidden away under the lining of the case. Apart from that, there was nothing else of any value to him and he stuffed the clothes into the hotel wardrobe, hopefully the maid would just think the woman was too lazy to bother hanging it all up. He brought the heavy bin bags out from the bathroom, he had tried his best to lighten their load, washing each part, ridding as much excess fluid as possible. Squashing and bending the awkward shapes without ripping the bags, he managed to get each piece into the suitcase, the head was the last to go in and caused an unsightly bulge as he zipped the case shut. Pulling it from the bed he was unable to soften it's journey to the floor, there was something about the dead, he could lift a person when they were stunned but as the life oozed out of them they became unmanageable. Heaving it onto it's side he discovered a small handle that lifted one end up, pushing the case onto wheels. He slung the holdall across his body, the hammer thumping a bruise into his hip, and made his way to the door. Sticking his head out he looked up and down the corridor, there was no sign or sound of anyone so as quickly as he could he half dragged, half rolled the heavy case into his room two doors along.

Now everything could be taken at his pace. Heaving the suitcase inside his wardrobe he closed the doors and fell backwards onto the soft double bed. The mattress gave way too easily to the contours of his body and the swirling seventies pattern on the quilted bedspread reminded him of car sickness as a child. Nevertheless, with the hardest part over and the opportunity to think about his next shopping trip, sleep placed a heavy hand across Matt's eyes pushing his mind down into a dreamless eight hours.

-15-

Guy

Guy slapped his face, his freshly shaven cheeks stung but it felt good. He sprayed deodorant under his arms then wiped his hands through his armpits and across his chest hair.

"They'll know you know." Lesley called from his bunk.

"What?" Guy feigned innocence.

"You fucking stink mate, no landscape fucking gardener goes to work stinking like that."

Guy stuck his head round the en-suite door, grinning at his cell mate. "So what if they do know. No-one does anything about it, they know it goes on and they also know it keeps the men happy. Happy prisoners, happy screws."

"It's getting a bit close to release date for you, don't fuck it up now." Lesley arched an eyebrow, a smirk pulling one side of his mouth up as his eyes caught Guy's.

"You, are just jealous mate, if a beautiful blonde offered to pick you up from work, drive you to a hotel and bang the living daylights out of you, you'd be smirking on the other side of your face."

Lesley turned back to the paperback held above him, "ah 'ave you forgotten the uncomplicated, professional services that the rest of us use? I thought all you aristocrats were the worst ones, all those deviant judges and politicians you know."

Guy ran a white and blue stripe of burning fresh toothpaste along his brush. "*If* I was from the aristocratic classes, which I'm not, I would take exception to your assumption that I might be deviant."

Lesley laughed, a great big raspy dirty guffaw. "You're posh you motherfucker, you're like one of those twisted snobs, you know, the ones that deny it. I've heard all about your folks."

Guy tried to speak through his foaming mouth, sticking his lower lip out to avoid dribbling on the floor. "My old man had to work for his money."

Lesley let his book slump onto his chest. "Aha, but *you've* got the silver spoon now."

"I give up."

"What was that mate?"

Guy took the toothbrush out of his mouth and stuck his head round the door again. "I said, I give up."

"Good, I'm always right." Lesley filled his lungs with air, rising his chest for maximum effect before lifting his book. "Anyhow, go off for your dial a fuck, I'm busy on higher things like this classic novel."

Guy sniffed his way through his wardrobe, searching for the freshest clothes whilst singing the ska version of "I'm in the Mood for Love", throwing occasional glances down at Lesley, who he knew, from the stationary position of his small beady eyes, was not reading but concentrating on ignoring him.

Finally, dressed and smelling good, he was ready. "Aren't you going to wish me luck then?"

The book went down yet again. "Go on, fuck off then, oh and by the way, you've got some post to pick up."

Guy stuck his head into the office on his way out, slinging an envelope with his mum's writing and another postcard from

Badger into his rucksack. Out front, his boss's van was waiting for him.

"Morning lover boy" he threw him a great big, brown skinned pikey grin "What time's she picking you up?"

Guy climbed into the front seat, squashing his rucksack into the dusty footwell. "Around midday"

"Good, I get a morning's work out of you first then eh!"

"This is going to be really embarrassing isn't it? I mean, they must know, I keep wondering if I should stay the night just so it looks less suspicious." Gina curled her slender arm around Guy's elbow, leaning her weight onto him as she wobbled up the hotel steps in her stiletto heels.

"Well, I should think they'll definitely guess with you wearing those shoes in the middle of the day. Either that or they'll think you're a prostitute."

Gina looked at him in horror, her eyes wide, the heavily mascaraed lashes like spider legs. "Oh god, you're right, I hadn't thought of that. I'm so stupid, I just wanted to make an effort for you, I wanted to fulfil a little male fantasy, after all, you've probably only been looking at girls in porno mags for the last couple of years."

Ridiculously, Guy felt slightly wounded. "Oh thanks, that's a bloody compliment."

Gina felt the tension run down his arm. "I'm sorry, I'm just nervous"

Guy stopped walking, standing just one step away from entering the hotel lobby, looking down at her petite face he felt mean. "It'll be fine, if it makes you feel any better, everyone comes here, all the wives and girlfriends, so the hotel's completely used to it. They probably rely on the prison for regular custom."

A small laugh forced it's way out of her. "I'm not sure that makes me feel any better. Okay, let's do it". She took a deep breath as they stepped into the revolving door, their hands touching as they pushed the brass bar until the merry go round spat them into the lobby. Gina looked at anything other than the clerk as Guy checked in. Casting her eyes over the polished space; even the over sized pot plants had glossy leaves, she noticed a couple tightly knotted around one another sitting on the soft lounge seats of the bar. They were both around forty, her mini skirt revealing the dimples of cellulite as her thigh crushed into her other leg in a bid to curl into her man. His large rough hand was resting between her legs, the fingers dangerously intimate, as he smiled a dark space was revealed where his canine tooth should have been. He was definitely from the prison. Gina was amazed at this whole other world going on that she had never been aware of before. Maybe her embarrassment was just naivety, looking back at the smiling face of the clerk, her hair tightly pulled into a French pleat, small pearl studs in the centre of her soft ear lobes, she wondered if this was all okay. Maybe the hotel really didn't mind, maybe this professional looking check in clerk was more aware of life's intricacies than she was. She managed to meet her eye and give a small smile. What did it matter, Guy was a beautiful looking man, she was so proud that he was hers, even if the woman guessed he was from the prison it probably wouldn't put her off him. Gina reckoned lots of girls would do the same.

Guy held her hand, giving it a very definite squeeze. "Okay honey, we're all checked in, shall we go up?" he pulled her gently from the desk and towards the corridor leading to two elevators "127."

"Uh huh", she scanned the brass numbers on the signs pointing the way to the lifts. With a ping the double door of one swooshed open, an older man stepped out, a newspaper folded under his arm, keeping his eyes on the floor he avoided acknowledging them.

Gina giggled, bumping her hip into Guy. "It wasn't his lucky day then."

Guy reached his arm out, pushing the button to keep the door open. "No, but I can't wait for mine." He pushed her into the lift, grabbing a buttock with each hand. She twisted from his grasp, turning into him as the door closed.

The sheets were crumpled in uncomfortable ridges under their bodies, the top sheet and blanket kicked down into a mound at the bottom of the bed, several cushions were scattered on the floor where Guy had needed padding for his knees. Gina pulled several tissues from the box beside the bed and squashed them between her legs, lying her head on his chest, she began to twist a finger through the short curls. "What are we going to do when you get out?"

He rolled over, pushing up onto his elbow, his other hand cupping her soft, falling breast, his thumb running back and forth across the nipple. "Go away somewhere"

"Where though? And what are we going to do when we get there? You must have ideas, you've had so much time to think about it."

"Yeah and I've also had a lot of time to realise that I just need to feel free for a little while."

She knew it was childish but couldn't help the little girly whine creep into her voice "Does that mean from me too?"

Guy laughed, looking into her eyes, a strange palette between hazel and green, pale jade with flecks of brown as if they hadn't yet decided what colour they were destined to be, the darker tones still waiting to spread and develop, they sat over a flat nose giving her the allure of a feline, her straight blonde hair fell across her mouth, half concealing the full lips that were currently puckered in a mild sulking expression. "No, of course not, look, maybe we could go here" he rolled over and lifted his backpack from the floor. Gina sat up, resting her back on the brown leather headboard and taking the opportunity to pull some of the crisp cotton sheet over her nakedness. Depositing grass clippings and a fine dusting of earth on the bed, Guy tipped the contents out, looking for the postcard. "Here."

Gina grabbed the glossy picture from him "What's this?" Turning it over she struggled to make sense of the childlike writing. "Impurtin trayde good. Life is lite. Wish you were here ☺ One day." She turned it over again, studying the photo, this time a deep, green bush clad mountain. "Who the hell is this?"

Guy laughed "He's an old cell mate, weird as fuck but he gets around, sends me postcards from all over the place."

"And you want to meet up with him?" Sarcasm dripped from her mouth.

"No, but I do want to get away, we've got time to think about it." Guy rolled out of the bed and walked into the en-suite, his conversation was accompanied by the heavy drum of pee jetting into the toilet bowl, "you've got no commitments, neither have I, let's enjoy being free agents for a while."

Gina lightly threw an "okay" towards him but secretly promised herself to work on a plan to calm the wanderlust in the gorgeous man relieving himself in the room next door. "What about your vineyard dream?"

Guy felt more than just relief in his bladder, the bathroom offered him some space, maybe he'd been inside for too long but he was struggling to cope with the idea of Gina being around all the time. Sat in the cell his heart had yearned for her, and not just sexually, he was sure he loved her. He'd got close to even considering marriage. The pain of loneliness inside prison walls slowly turned into something more sour, bitterness, paranoia even anger. He could see it all around him and had tried desperately to keep his insides soft, daydreams of a wife, maybe even children had protected the tender part of his soul. Now, as he looked down at the yellow toilet bowl and the end of his cock turning pink from too much sex, he wondered if it had just been romantic foolishness and he really was just destined to be on his own.

"I haven't forgotten it, it's a huge commitment, it would take every penny I've put aside, I want to make sure I'm ready to settle when I do it."

Gina curled out of the bed and creaked open the wooden wardrobe, a thick white towelling dressing gown slipped off the blonde wooden hanger. It was too big and too thick for her warm body, a dry layer of sweat lay on her skin making her feel dirty. She tied it round her waist and walked to the en-suite. Guy was bending over the bath squeezing a small plastic bottle under the running tap, the contents thin and yellow, more like washing up liquid than anything she wanted her skin soaking up.

"I thought the vineyard idea sounded perfect. You wouldn't have to work a nine to five, you could walk around bare foot, the sun on your back, living in harmony with the seasons."

Guy continued to stare into the water. "It's not all about the land. There would be a business end to it as well. Wine is just as much about the scientists nowadays, then there's marketing to consider, it's an international competitive industry."

Gina slid her arm under Guy's stomach, his muscles puckering upwards at the touch. "But that's where I come in surely? You know I'm experienced in marketing, I enjoy that side of things, you could work outside and I can take care of the office."

The arm was gently persuading Guy to stand up and turn to her. "Let's just have a bit of down time first that's all I'm saying, I'm not sure how my head is going to respond to freedom."

Maybe if they travelled together he would get used to sharing his space with her, he really didn't want to be on his own anymore.

-16-

Matthew

The school railings were so hot they shimmered, Matthew wilted as he stood beside them. The playground was empty, the concrete beating under the sun, lifeless like some Moon training ground. He stood apart, although his Spanish was getting better, he just wasn't in the mood to make the extra effort required to converse with the other waiting parents. He needed thinking time, cash flow was beginning to dry up again. A few of the more predatory women watched him, he felt their eyes undressing him. He knew they what they wanted, he was in better shape than most of their husbands, and a lot better off. They laughed at his English accent, a couple of them would even touch, a casual hand on his arm, an elbow in his ribs. Finally, the school bell bounced around the stone walls and the quiet building sprung to life. Through the open windows the sounds of chairs being scraped back, the raised voices of teachers trying to be heard over the children's din. The large blue wooden doors creaked open and a stream of kids tumbled through and down the steps onto the playground. They all carried non-uniform backpacks like a crowd of Disney tortoises. Matt scanned the colourful swarm for Philly. He thought she was so special and yet found her difficult to find in the crowd. She spotted him first.

"Hola Matty!"

He looked down at the round brown face, her eyes twinkling with excitement. "Are you taking me for ice cream?"

He stroked the top of her head, her black hair smooth and warm. "I promised your mum I'd get a chicken for dinner, let's go to the market."

Matthew always struggled not to fill his stomach at the food market. The greasy aroma of fresh tacos and fried pork rind threatened to ruin his appetite for dinner. The stalls bustled with women buying produce, their voices thrown over the sacks and containers as they haggled with the owners. Accompanying children would often suffer slapped hands as their tempted fingers wormed into the large open bags of candid fruits. Matthew struggled to keep his eye on Philly.

She skipped ahead of him, occasionally disappearing as bodies crowded between them.

"Philly, *Philly!*" Looking over people's shoulders he could just make out the top of her black head. She spun round, her ponytail swinging into the side of her face, her forehead creased as she searched the faces behind her. Her eyes caught his and her mouth opened, a gappy, toothy grin.

"Stay with me, it's busy today."

"Okay Matty." Her hand slipped inside his, he marvelled at how easy she found the intimate gesture.

"Look, the Polleria." She tugged him over to the poultry stall. Rows of yellow plucked chickens hung their limp heads over the edge of the stand. "Can I choose?"

"Course."

She bent over, looking up at the heads dangling above her. Matthew could swear she was talking to them. The stall holder lost interest and moved to serve another customer.

"This one." Philly placed a finger under the beak, raising the chicken's head until it looked at Matthew.

"What's special about this one?"

"Well, he looks a bit sad and I think if we eat him then he'll feel his life wasn't wasted."

He could hear the language of Nieve in his little girl's grown up philosophy. "Okay, that's the one for us then."

The aproned stall holder nodded and grabbed the dead animal by it's feet. "Desea que preparara?"

"No, gracias." Matthew could do it himself.

Philly had left his side again, across the aisle ensconced in a stall bursting with colour. Vases of fake flowers; blue chrysanthemums, red roses; balanced atop neatly folded Mexican striped blankets. Baskets of earthenware mugs sat amid cooking pots filled with wooden spoons. Philly had moved from the street, under the canopy and into the darker depths of the stall. Lining the back wall religious icons smiled beatifically down on them. Christ hung from the cross a multitude of times. Matthew noticed how the eyes still held sadness, an element of emotion that simply didn't exist once the body was dead. If he wasn't hanging from a cross than he was staring into space, his hands resting in prayer. Matthew guessed it was to show forgiveness, forgiving the bastards that stuck him on the cross even. In the centre of all the wooden and stone figures, an angel smiled at Matthew. Her small head covered by a long blue cape, a golden crown seemingly suspended above it, rays spread from her body, little stems that ended in stars. A pink gown fell to the ground, folds gathered round her feet. She too, had her hands clasped in prayer but her look was of love. Pure love. She stared at Matthew. She looked inside him, saw everything and still loved him.

"Nuestra Senora de Guadeloupe." Philly joined him.

"Huh?"

"Our Lady of Guadeloupe." Philly translated.

"Oh yes, I've heard of her."

"Have you seen the cloak?"

"What cloak?" Matthew looked at his daughter. Of course, Nieve would have brought her up Catholic.

"The one she gave Juan Diego. To show us all. It has her picture on it, it's hundreds of years old and you can still see it."

"Wow, she must be very special."

"Yes, she protects us, just like a real mum but one for everybody."

Matthew looked back to the porcelain face. "Do you think she'd protect me?"

"Yes, everyone, she loves everybody."

"What about bad people?"

"That's not her job, to judge I mean. You know the golden rule?"

Matthew remembered Nieve teaching him something but he couldn't recall exactly what it was about. "No."

"Do unto others as you would have them do unto you. What we do, God will do to us. So, you see, it's not our Lady's job to decide if you're a goodie or a badie." Philly's eagerness to prove her knowledge pleased Matthew.

"Do you like her? The statue I mean."

"She's very pretty." Philly ran a finger around the gold base. It struck Matthew as a very glamorous object, certainly not like the humble shepherd's surrounding them.

"Let's take her home, your mum'll be very proud of us."

Philly smiled, "Can I carry her?"

"Course, but we've got to get a move on, this chicken is going to start smelling soon.""

Matthew placed the Virgin on a shelf that ran along the back wall of the living room. He pushed Nieve's vases and books to the edge and his Lady took the most central position. Nothing was allowed to touch her; she needed her own space. When the sun shone through the courtyard doors, rays would catch the golden stars and little circles of light travelled around the wooden floor. They ate, watched tele, argued and laughed underneath her watchful gaze. Every morning he would look at her, just a quick acknowledgement at the start of each day. The Virgin was there for him, filling a space left by his parents. It was frustrating that he couldn't take her when he travelled, maybe he could look for a small replica that would fit neatly in a suitcase. Whenever he doubted himself, or was troubled by the heaviness inside him, he could look at that beautiful face and know he wasn't alone.

Another trip. Nieve hadn't questioned him this time. He knew she wasn't stupid, sat behind the till all day she was well aware that the shop didn't bring in enough to justify their lifestyle. He'd told her he was sourcing pieces in South East Asia for a client, it wasn't that hard to believe, she knew he still had an interest in the antiques trade and she also knew that he had old contacts in that part of the world. She'd accepted his explanation, even if she had doubts. The reality was he needed to put some miles under his belt, he'd done quite a few lately and wasn't confident that he could keep getting away with it so close to home. He knew no-one suspected anything but it was better to stay ahead of the field, working across continents should ensure complete safety. He was gonna stay away a bit longer this time, get a few done. Philly was needing more, they hadn't yet had the 'father' conversation, Nieve still prickled every time he mentioned it, but he was certain she was his. After all, why would Nieve let him get so close to her otherwise? And she was bright, sharp and he wanted her to get the best education. He wasn't going to see her struggle away like him, a second class bloody citizen, but it needed money, lots of it. The best schools didn't come cheap and nothing else was going to be good enough for his little princess. He closed his eyes, listening to the hum and drone of the plane's engines. He'd got some new equipment for this trip, things were going to run more smoothly than ever. There was always the painful nugget of fear that his luggage might get searched at the airport but the whole butchery thing could explain the majority of his tools. He was on a roll, a quick stop over in Singapore and he'd accomplished one already. A big American bastard, it had been a bit too quick really, no time to look for a decent place to dump the body. The hotel sat along a river which ran to the sea, and that had to do. He'd got this flight out the next day, a bit of distance in that respect anyway. In the air again he felt like a being set apart, hovering above the world, dropping down and making a connection, someone offering themselves to him and then, whoosh, up in the air again, disappearing, an invisible force. He'd made a couple of connections with people on the plane already and was going to continue warming them up when they reached the airport, he'd have plenty of time while they waited for their luggage.

Matt sat down on the curved metal seat of the Bangkok arrivals hall. His jaw was tense in anger, his teeth grinding, nothing had worked. Two of them had rejected him, wasted his fucking time. He watched the movement of human traffic, trolleys loaded up with cases, meandering their way through the crowds. He kept trying to pick one out from the herd, the weaker ones, looking bewildered, lonely, their pace slightly slower as they scanned for information, talking to themselves, but it was no use. His mood had left him, depression sat on him like a dark hat and no-one in their right mind would trust him now. The darkness gnawed at his insides and he knew he would have to do something to shake it, problem was he now couldn't achieve his usual fix and would have to battle it away by pure will power, forcing it down, allowing the sunny nature to cloak him and attract his next conquest. Maybe he should give up on the city and head towards one of the tourist resorts, at least they were there in numbers and it would just be a matter of identifying someone with a small shadow that he could adhere to.

265 Dirty Luggage

He wheeled his case to the flight desk and booked on the next available flight to a popular tourist haunt. Maybe the therapy of beautiful beaches would serve to clear his head.

His feet broke the top crust of the white sand, like icing, they than sank into the soft powder, his thigh muscles straining as he walked along with his legs in a constantly bent position. The ocean curled into a long wave that crashed in a line running the length of the gently curved bay. The noise a rhythmic pounding that started in front of him and continued past, like a distant thunder roll behind him. Rock formations sat in the ocean like sharp conical islands, the sunlight creating shadows on the limestone, dark ledges that sea birds landed on, their large white wings flapping as they dropped themselves down. White foam crashed around the islands, swirling over invisible rocks, warning swimmers not to come to close. Two neon yellow snorkels stuck out from the turquoise shallows, their owners lying stationary over dark purple blobs of underwater rocks and seaweed, the marine life attracted to the nooks and crevices. Matt walked towards the cliff face that circled the end of the bay, small trees clung to the edges, their roots grey and twisted as they struggled to keep a hold on the crevasses that offered a little soil and water. He could see two brown bodies lying next to one another behind one of the large rocks that appeared to have dropped from the cliff. It stopped him going any closer, he didn't want to intrude. Lying his towel on the dry sand he twisted his sunnies off and turned to the ocean. Waiting for the wave to pass him he strode quickly into the warm water, as it climbed towards his navel he dived in. Feeling the water washing over his head he tried to cleanse the darkness from him, his eyes ached through lack of sleep and as he surfaced he lifted his face to the sun, feeling the burn on the shadows under his sore eyes. Spotting the hump of rising water on his close horizon, his legs feeling the suck of the growing wave, he turned to face the shore, positioning himself for a fast front crawl, propelling into the churning sand as the wave lifted and then tumbled him into the foam. Standing up he noticed the brightly painted 'Scuba Diving' sign that had been slapped onto the side of a scruffy white square stone building. A reassuring PADI flag flapped from the corner and a small group of western looking tourists were sat on the window ledge outside, back packs and SCUBA bags in a pile on the pavement. Matt felt his head clear, new energy awoke his senses. It was inspiration, dive boats were renowned for their sociability, so much so, that many carried lone travellers.

He kept both hands on the bench as the boat hit the small waves, rocking and bumping the twelve passengers. Several couples were on the boat, engrossed in their own company, Matt hadn't bothered to strike up conversation. He'd heard one young bloke with an English accent but he looked more like a backpacker, in his early twenties, hair frazzled and sun damaged, a coarse, bristly growth of hair bursting from his tanned face. He had already made a buddy of another backpacker who Matt guessed, from his deep throated pronunciation of English, was French. There was one possibility left. At the end of the opposite bench, the rack of tanks between them, sat a very white looking middle aged man. His fair hair was conservatively short, standing upright in the wind from the boat. He looked quite geeky, his slim body sliding comfortably into a pair of Speedos. The good thing, Matt noticed, was he had all his own equipment, new and a good quality brand. He'd watched him fitting his BCD onto the tank, slotting his own weights into the jacket. His attention was now focused on the dive computer strapped to the slim wrist, his soft nailed fingers working different combinations of buttons accompanied by different lengths of beeps. After configuring whatever program he was fiddling with, he took the wire framed glasses off his face, folding them carefully and placing them into a hard case in the dive bag pushed under the bench beneath him. All Matt needed now was to hear him speak. As if God was listening, the dive guide stepped out from the cockpit with a clipboard in her hand. With the borderline emaciation of all dive instructors, she was cool enough to have a full length wet suit pulled up to her waist already. She cast a look along both benches and then began to speak to each person, organising the buddy system, making sure each diver was partnered up with someone. She crouched in front of the opposite bench first and discovered that Markus who was Dutch but spoke English fluently, was on his own. She then stood up and approached Matt.

"Hi, you must be Jerry."

Matt looked up at the deeply tanned girl, her hair lay in two plaits that just touched the top of her yellow bikini, the triangles almost flat against her slim chest. He pushed his Ray Bans on to the top of his head and gave a cheek slicing smile.

"Yes."

"Okay Jerry, if it's okay with you, I'm gonna team you up with Markus over there. If you guys can get on with sorting out your equipment and have a quick buddy run through, hand signals and what not, we've got another twenty minutes or so. I'll give everyone a briefing in about five, okey dokey?"

Matt tried to suppress the urge to reply okily dokily and instead squeezed his lips together and nodded. Markus had been watching all the time and seeing his cue moved across the boat, with one hand for support on the bench he raised the other to Matt in a handshake.

"Hello, I'm Markus, we're buddies right?"

"Yes, call me Jerry." And Matt held the long fingered hand of his new friend.

They'd made arrangements to meet up for a drink, Matt was going to impart some local knowledge to the Dutchman who had just completed a business deal and was keen to grab a few days r and r before heading home.

Matt hadn't been in the country long enough for his nose to de-sensitise to the waft of drains mixed with the sweet scent of the joss sticks that were positioned in the little offerings laid out by the locals. Little square parcels were found in unexpected places, thick, fleshy petaled flowers, rice wrapped in shiny banana leaves. One of the little offerings was placed on the bottom of the stone step leading to the hotel. Two huge Hindu statues danced on either side of the entrance, the twisted hands of Shiva the gold paint of his headdress reflecting the sun, a bright light in the dim shade of the cool lobby. An enormous ceiling fan scuttled the leaves across the polished marble floor, small birds had found safety in the exposed rafters, their song a pleasant tinkle almost designed to fit in with the ambience of the hotel. Matt quickly scanned for room signs and followed a corridor off to the right, broken shiny legs and the crunchy body parts of cockroaches were swept into the edges of the tiled floor. Matt laughed to himself, he could probably get a job as a hotel inspector nowadays. The contents of his holdall had shifted slightly and a clinking noise accompanied his strides, placing a hand against it, he squashed the bag into his leg. The corridor led through an outdoor courtyard, a gentle gurgle filled the space from a water feature in the centre, a stone fish was forever leaping upwards, a trickle of water spurted from it's mouth and dribbled into the pool. Singular, large tropical flowers lifted their trumpet shaped heads to the sky, ready to fill up with the warm rain before it ran over the deep green glossy leaves. Passing through the humid space, Matt entered the cool interior that led to Markus's room. His heart rate began to increase as he visualised his plan, like an actor practicing his lines behind the curtain.

He knocked twice, made of a mahogany coloured hard wood the door left his knuckles feeling tender. The door opened fully and Markus filled the space. Matt stepped forward quickly, forcing the smaller man to step sideways, allowing Matt to enter the room.

"What a great bed, I haven't stayed here before, I must remember it, it's a nice hotel don't you think?" Matt had walked into the centre of the room, standing at the bottom of a king sized bed, four black wooden posts rose from each corner.

"Ah, yes." Markus closed the door, accepting that his guest was obviously going to stay for a minute before they left.

"What's the view like?" Matt looked at Markus before walking slowly towards the French doors, the louver shutters half open. Markus took the bait, moving to the window, he turned his back to Matt as he pushed the bifold doors fully open. Matt's hand dove swiftly into the holdall, drawing out the stun gun in one flowing movement. Just as Markus began to turn his head to face Matt, the gun walloped him in the side of the head, sending wave after wave of electricity through his mind. Markus crumpled and began to fall heavily, his head smashing into the arm of the Balinese armchair, his gold framed spectacles bending before they slid off the end of his nose. A complete dead weight, Markus's head hit the floor with a heavy thud. Matt threw the bag onto the ground, dropping to his knees beside Markus he rummaged through it's contents, looking for his new purchase. A sound erupted from the stunned man's throat, an involuntary groan as the air escaped his convulsing body. Matt looked with surprise at the jerking man, this hadn't happened before, Markus's eyes looked glazed, exactly like that of a dead cow, his lips were bouncing off one another, almost like blowing a raspberry, saliva ran constantly from the corner of his mouth, along his cheek and onto the floor. His arms were clasped in front of him, his legs kicking in and out of the foetal position, . The convulsing finally stopped and Matt noticed Markus's brown eyes begin to shift, trying to gain focus. Shit, he was coming round. He was determined not to kill him here, he had to find the handcuffs. Finally he felt the circular metal of his new quick cuffs, the wrists opened as you slammed them onto your captive's arms. He knelt over the dazed man and rolled him face down into the carpet, yanking his arms behind him. Just as the cuffs closed around the slim wrists, he felt Markus buck his body. He was totally conscious and wanting to fight. Matt squeezed the metal of the cuffs tight to the point of producing red wheals around the white skin. Markus attempted to shout, his voice muffled by the carpet. Matt leant over, grabbing the fallen stun gun, administering another violent charge to the back of Markus's head. Again the convulsing started and Matt quickly stood up, moving away from the violently kicking legs. After a minute the convulsing stopped and he risked grabbing the, now, limp ankles, dragging Markus towards the bathroom. The man's skin squeaked as his face was dragged over the marble floor and he began to make small grunting noises again. Matt flicked the light switch, the hum of the extractor fan conveniently loud enough to cover the sounds emitting from Markus. Leaping over the trussed body, Matt ran back through the bedroom and picked up the holdall. With the mallet in his hand he walked back into the brightly lit bathroom. Markus had managed to turn himself over, on seeing the large hammer in Matt's hands, fear screamed through his eyes as his mouth gibbered uselessly. He tried raising his legs in an effort to kick out at his attacker but the shocks had taken all the strength from his body, a cold slick of perspiration clung to his face and the saliva gathered in his mouth, a dangerous swirl before vomiting. Matt planted a powerful kick into Markus's groin, causing the stricken man to pull his legs up in defence. Able to get closer Matt then leant down, grabbing the fabric of the t-shirt on Markus's right shoulder, heaving him up before twisting him over onto his face again. Markus tried to resist, his muscles straining to keep himself facing his attacker. Matt placed a foot in the middle of his back, forcing the wriggling body down. He raised the hammer and let the full, heavy force, swing into the back of Markus's head.

The SCUBA bag was perfect. He pushed all the body parts, slippery inside their bin bags, and then attempted to hoist it onto his shoulders, even with both hands bringing the handles up his back he knew it was going to be virtually impossible to carry the weight all the way through the hotel and to the hire car. He wanted the bag though, he had studied the map in the rental car and new of a few well scattered areas to deposit the body parts. He was hoping that he could keep the dive bag afterwards. He'd have to use the bloke's Samsonite suitcase as well, but it was a bugger trying to get rid of the hard cases, it would have to go into water, loaded down. As he looked out to the balcony, another message was sent to him. The BCD, dive vest, was sitting on the concrete floor drying. Squeezing his fingers into the cold wet pockets he pulled out the dive weights.

He rolled the suitcase along the floor and hitched the SCUBA bag over his shoulder. Shaking with exertion he tried to give the impression of ease as he walked through the lobby. A porter, smiling brown face underneath a burgundy pill box hat, approached him, his hands outstretched. "Let me help you sir."

"Oh no, it's quite all right thank you, my car is just outside." But the desire to please was to strong for the tip motivated young man.

"Oh no, please, please." and he placed his hand on the centre handle of the suitcase.

Oh well, thought Matthew, there was just no stopping some people, and so, together they walked to the little white hatchback. Fishing in his trouser pocket, he pulled out a crumpled note, pressing it into the man's hand before he could offer to lift the case into the boot.

"Thank you sir." And with a little nod, his helpful friend retreated back to the shade of the hotel.

Adrenalin coursed through his veins. This was always the riskiest part. The darkness offered him a cloak but it also made navigation more difficult. The town's lights were well behind him and he relied solely on the headlights of the car as the gravel road swung heavily left and right, winding it's way through the peaks and valley's of the hills. It had to be taken slowly, to misjudge one of the bends would send the car nose diving into pure darkness, crashing through the dense canopy. A curved cut out offered respite for driver's needing to pull over. It was just what he was looking for.

Away from any light pollution the night sky was thick, soft, black velvet. The moon cast a blue white glow over the car, Matt's hands looked ghostly as he unzipped the dive bag. The boot had hummed with the smell of the body but as the bag was opened all the trapped odours escaped, Matt screwed his nostrils and breathed sideways as he stuck his fingernails into the black plastic bags, tearing them open. Like pulses of electricity, the jungle buzzed with the chirruping songs of thousands of freaky looking bugs, Matt bent and ducked at the waist, avoiding brushing any branches, his skin crawled just thinking about the long spiky legs that might scuttle around the neck of his t-shirt. He threw the butchered body parts into the valley, sailing through the dark foliage the skin looked stark white, the bloodied ends black, until distant crashes as they disappeared through the tree canopies. It wouldn't take long for the fat jungle rats to find his waste.

Turning the car around, he headed back into the town. A deep river ran from the mountains, under a bridge and into the sea. It was a perfect destination for the suitcase but he'd need to work quickly, he'd be exposed on the bridge. As the car hit the smooth tarmac he could see the large square headlights of a truck approaching in the other direction. If he drove slowly enough, it would pass before he left the bridge. A check in the rear view mirror showed nothing but darkness. With one hand on the gear stick he braked hard, throwing the vehicle into park, it wobbled to a stop and then he yanked up the handbrake. Leaning down he popped the lever for the boot and, leaving the car door open and the engine running, he ran round to the back. He dragged the heavy suitcase out, allowing it to fall onto the ground, then scraped it across to the gutter. Squatting down, placing his hands under the case, he heaved it up the protective metal barrier, trying to keep his back straight and his thighs strained. A final, muscle trembling shove upwards and it tipped over. A moment's silence and then a heavy plop, a reassuring deep sound.

Sweating but smiling, Matt thumped the boot down and jumped into the driver's seat, his stomach lurched and wobbled in a hungry rumble, he always forgot to eat while he was working. It was time to get back to his hotel and order some room service.

The plastic card slid smoothly into the door and with a beep and little flash of green, the latch clicked open. Sitting on the end of the bed he unlaced his trainers, his feet warm and swollen, were dying to feel fresh air. Pulling off the thick sports socks he noticed a tiny dot of blood on the rubber edge of his left shoe, never mind, he always chucked his shoes after each job anyway. He'd learnt from bitter experience that trainers, with their multitude of seams and cracks, were experts at hiding blood. He'd tried scrubbing them clean in the past but was never convinced that they were clear, he knew that modern forensics could detect the tiniest spec and so, from then on, he'd decided a new pair of trainers was a decent reward each time he'd completed a job. Picking them up he threw the barely worn, Nike shoes nose down into the small round bin, the maid would probably take them for a son or husband. Picking up the menu he scanned the list of options, a strange mixture of western favourites, Mediterranean influences and then a couple of local dishes. It was probably better to choose the local options, they would be better cooked as they knew what to do with them. A steaming plate of noodles, egg and meats would line his stomach beautifully before sleep. Holding the menu, he noticed the dry black blood underneath his thumbnails, he would order and then jump under a shower while he waited.

-17-

Singapore, 1995

Staff Sergeant Lee was excited, nervous, but generally excited. This is why she joined CID, not for the tedious fraud investigations, or the vicious assaults that drug dealers committed on one another. No, murder, homicide, that was what you trained for. And not the emotional impulsive domestic kind either but, a cold blooded, sickening murderer, the sort of person that you couldn't believe you were sitting in the same room as, the kind of person you wanted to dig deeper into, wondering how on earth they managed to grow into someone that could quite calmly snuff out human life for their own ends. Hopefully, in the end, having the satisfaction of seeing justice served on them, knowing, with a clean conscience that it was the best thing, that they truly deserved no place amongst normal society.

A fisherman had hooked out two bin bags from the Singaporean waters. As they had flumped onto the deck a nauseating smell had scared the old man and he made his way back to the pier before opening them. As he rolled one of the bags over, trying to find the knot, several human toes peeked out of the opening at him. He hollered to his mate to contact the coastguard, there was no bloody way he was opening the bag.

Sergeant Lee pulled her car into the bays outside the marina's office. It was seven thirty in the morning, the sun was just beginning to warm the sky, seagulls barked their calls above her head, they were on the alert for returning fishing boats. At the end of the pier she could see the small trawler, the Coastguards white shirt gleaming next to the loose, dirty clothing of the two fishermen. She walked along the wooden deck, her creaking footsteps alerting the three men of her arrival. The Coastguard held his arm out to her, helping her step across and onto the stinking fish boat. No-one said a word, at their feet lay two plastic bin bags, torn open, lying on one a rubbery mass of flesh falling away from the long, heavy bones of a human leg. The other was so gruesome that no dark humour could be found to ease it's impact. A human head, decomposing, the soft flesh eaten by fish. Two dark holes stared at them, the eyeballs missing. The mouth and nose fleshless spaces, an expression of pure horror, the brown hair strangely vibrant on top of the grotesque white skull. The remnants of the neck skin like a frilled skirt beneath the head.

Sergeant Lee returned to her car, pulling out her go bag, full of statement forms, evidence bags and gloves. She had called for back up in the form of colleagues for statement taking, and the search team to work alongside the Coastguard. Her Superintendent would meet her at the morgue, the pathologist had been alerted and would be treating it as a priority. She made a mental note to buy some extra strong mints on the way to the morgue. She did not want to risk looking queasy in front of her superior.

With the evidence bags in the boot of her vehicle she headed to the mortuary.

Sitting on the metal table the two parts seemed inconsequential. Lee was more used to the floppy mass of a full body, in comparison, the head and the leg looked like rotten, chewed up chunks of meat sitting in a butcher's window. The strip lighting; so bright and evenly spread that no shadow was allowed to fall; the circular drains imbedded in the smooth floor and the sterile, stainless steel tables, in this clinical and impersonal environment, were still unable to mask the putrefying smell. Even a post mortem on the recently dead was hard enough to stomach, let alone the smell of these crawling pieces of meat. She sucked hard on the large white mint, it's cool, almost burning sensation, numbing her mouth and a waft of menthol cleared her head. The Superintendent was leaning right over the table, following the pointer of the pathologist, the two men's heads covered by the protective headwear, like shower caps. Lee preferred to stand at the end, watching proceedings from an arm's length. Sometimes it paid more to listen, the pathologist had the air of a surgeon, an aloofness that Lee felt slightly intimidating, his cool eyes rested on a serious face, there was no funeral house laughter allowed here. Her Superintendent was eager to learn, his interest in all disgusting matters was like music to the pathologist's ears, an opportunity for him to demonstrate his knowledge. The Super was busy studying the smooth bone protruding from the lower leg, the point at which the knee should sit, and then Lee heard a comment that was to continually repeat itself in her mind.

"Mmm, yes, it's interesting isn't it, normally you would see striations on the bone, a lot of hacking when someone tries to chop up a body. In my opinion, you will be looking for someone that knows how to dis-articulate joints" the Super looked up at the serious face across the table from him. "Go on."

"Well, by that I mean, you can assume that you are looking for a trained person, professions that require a good knowledge of anatomy and joints."

Lee stepped closer, watching her Superintendent form the next question.

"Like a doctor?"

"More like a surgeon, a vet or a butcher."

A few things were on their side. The victim was a white, male of European appearance, that narrowed the search, possibly a tourist or one of the ex-pats. They also had a fascinating insight into the profession or training of the killer. Lee's first task was to search the Missing Person records, thankfully she didn't have to go back to far the death had probably only occurred a week or so ago. As she flipped through the first batch of reports a photo jumped out at her, an attractive white face with a mop of brown hair, a faxed copy of a report filed in the US, Mr Aaron Philips. Mrs Philips was worried for the welfare of her husband. He had left the family home ten days ago for a quick business trip to Singapore. He had not been heard of since, and that, she insisted, was completely out of character. It had not been pursued as his credit card had been in use and money transfers had taken place, the assumption being that he was still alive and well somewhere but, his particulars matched the distorted parts in the mortuary perfectly, right age, right height, right ethnicity. She left the filing room and walked back to the CID office, the Super was copying from his notebook a list of tasks to be completed onto the large white board fixed to the wall. Detectives sat at desks ill designed to cope with computers, court files, telephones and boxes of evidence. Bags of equipment cluttered the walking space between and the general impression was of industrious chaos.

"Excuse me sir?" The Super turned round, his marker pen hovering in the air.

"I think I've identified a possible victim."

He took the piece of A4 paper from her, his smile broadening as he read the details.

"I think you're going to need to phone the family, we're going to require a DNA sample."

Lee gulped, next of kin calls were the absolute downside to the job, whatever department you were in.

"Yes sir."

"Well done Lee." And he gave a reassuring look that understood the horrible conversation she was about to have.

The missing person's elderly father was arranging to have a DNA swab taken with his local police, they would then engineer it's transport from the US over to Singapore. Lee put the phone down with a heavy heart, that poor family, he had a baby son as well. Looking out the window she could just make out the haze of blue sea between the high rises, somewhere the rest of this man's body was floating.

-18-

Matthew, Bangkok

"Hey baby, how you doing?" Matt rolled on to his side, the springy telephone wire bouncing on his lips as they moved.

Nieve smiled, he sounded warm and happy, he must be doing well. "Hello Matty, how are you?"

"I'm good beautiful. Tell Philly that daddy will be bringing home a surprise."

Nieve looked out to the courtyard, her darling girl was squatting on her haunches stroking a skinny black cat, arching it's back, desperate to reach the soft hand caressing it. "Oh Matty, you give too much, she got so much, don't go crazy." She kind of meant it and kind of didn't. It was so nice to be spoiled, so warming not to have to worry about money. Matt laughed, he could just picture her face, her forehead puckered into a frown, trying to appear serious but the corners of her mouth just twinkling upwards. "And you Nievey, I've got things for you to."

Nieve curled her legs underneath her, making herself comfortable to enjoy the phone call "Oh Matty, what have you got me?"

"I'm not telling you, you'll have to wait, but it's all good Nievey, I'm doing really well, it's been a good trip."

She wanted to lean into his voice, soak up the deep tones that soothed her loneliness "When are you coming home Matty?"

"Soon Nievey, soon. I've got a little more to do then I'll be back, just another week."

The ache in her chest threatened to twist into tears. "I miss you." And her breath caught in her throat, the words left hanging in the air.

"I know baby girl, don't you worry, I'll be home soon and it will all be good. Look, I've got to go, I'm on a hotel phone, it'll cost a bloody fortune."

"Where are you Matty?"

Matt rolled onto his back noticing several dead flies trapped in the glass of the uplighters on the wall above his bed.

He exhaled deeply. "I'm all over the place, got associates I need to catch up with. Don't worry, I'll be home soon."

Nieve's legs stretched along the sofa, her head resting on the arm. "Okay, okay Matty, just call me okay?"

"Yep, will do, speak soon."

"Bye Matty."

Matthew rolled over and pulled the bedside drawer open. In the absence of his Lady, he had taken to inspirational readings from the bibles provided in hotel rooms.

'Be strong and courageous. Do not be afraid or terrified because of them, for the LORD your God goes with you; he will never leave you nor forsake you.'

Deutoronomy 31:6

Matthew smiled to himself, no need to look again. The vibrations of bus engines intruded through the net curtains and into his room, the overnight rain had saturated the morning air, washing away the pollution but enhancing the sounds of the traffic swishing through the city. If he got a move on he might just make breakfast, he was still hungry and his head was sending daggers across the backs of his eyes. Food and a strong coffee might evaporate the sharp hooks that were clinging to his eyelids.

Feeling comfortable; clean, fresh and charged with caffeine, Matt wandered slowly through the hotel foyer. A mound of suitcases cluttered the marble floor, gathered together, like a small herd, safety in numbers, their owners killing time before the coach arrived to bustle them away from their holiday and back to the familiarity of home. Matt felt the luxury of having no commitments easing a space inside him, like a warm friend shouldering their way inside his mind, occupying pleasant and relaxed territory. In the corner, beside a large potted palm, a white board was covered with the squeaky writing of a marker pen *Welcome, please talk to our tour representative. We are here to help.* Behind the empty desk tour leaflets decorated the wall, smiling faces on theme park rides, zoo animals photographed to look like close encounters, smiling Thai faces inviting you to eat in their traditional restaurants and in the centre, a white woman, laughing and balancing on the back of an elephant, the jungle dense and dark behind her. Matthew reached out to pull the leaflet from it's plastic shelf. A young, suntanned, female hand brushed his, reaching for the exact same information.

"Oh, I'm sorry." And the hand retracted swiftly. Matt turned to the sweet Canadian voice. She was attractive in that sort of, sensible, sporty, timeless way. Her hair was combed off her face and twisted into a half pony tail, golden highlights ran through it matching the blonde hairs on her arms. She had the look of someone who had spent a long time on a sandy beach, twenty something, maybe a cannabis smoking backpacker, the type who wore twisted friendship bracelets until it was time to return home, swap the jandals for shoes and take up the profession they had studied for. Except, she was staying here, an international standard hotel and, Matt noticed quickly, she was wearing diamond studs, heavy enough that they just turned their heads to the floor.

"It's okay, great minds think alike eh?" And he smiled at her, running his hand through the flop of hair on his forehead.

"After working hard I've found myself with a little time to kill and this looks like fun doesn't it?"

"Yes." She returned his smile, her perfect white teeth enhancing the tan on her face, freckles danced softly across her nose and the tops of her cheeks. "Have you done it before?"

"Yes, and it's worth doing again, if nothing else it gets you away from the city and the tourist beaches, you get to bathe with the elephants too."

She laughed, a sociable, trusting bubble. "Sounds like fun. We flew up from Phuket a couple of days ago and now we're looking to get away from the city. I'd like to get to the rainforest before we go home."

Matt scanned the space behind her, another attractive twenty something man was just leaving the dining room. "Your husband?"

She looked behind her, catching the man's attention and waving him over. "Yes."

Matt took the opportunity to look at her left hand, the thumb tucked into the waistband of her yellow and white surfers shorts. A wedding band and solitaire diamond engagement ring shone brightly from the honey coloured skin. It had the gun metal look of platinum. The young man walked over, loose drawstring linen trousers hung folded at his ankles, brown toes spread comfortably in leather sandals, a surfing style vest top revealed well defined shoulders. Matt guessed he was a footballer, trimmed down by his time travelling Asia. He slipped a strong arm around the waist of the girl, pressing his lips into her cheek.

"Hello darling."

"Hi babe, we were just talking about the elephant trekking, this is.. I'm sorry, we don't know each other's name!"

Matt held his hand out to the husband. "Jerry, pleased to meet you"

With one arm still wrapped territorially around his wife, the husband extended his other. "Brett, and this is my wife Jules" Matt shook the offered hand, staring into the face of this other man. His hair was shaved almost bald, he had a strong jaw line and well defined cheekbones. His smile was not as open as his wife's but Matt guessed that was just his boring jealousy, Jules was attractive and probably got a lot of very interested male attention. It struck Matt that he could be standing in front of a couple straight off a factory line, their bodies young and healthy, their bones strong, teeth gleaming in fleshy skin, their minds educated in good schools, training them for middle class professions before the suburban home and children arrived. Their class and wealth were displayed in the little pieces of glass dotted around the woman's body, her earrings, her wedding rings. Their luggage probably carried motifs, similar to the labels in their clothing. Was it a sign? He hadn't been thinking of taking on more than one person at a time but this seemed to be an opportunity designed for him. Was God testing him? Asking him if he was ready, was he masterful enough? Or maybe God already knew that and was offering it to him so obviously that he couldn't fail to notice. It would take planning, these two people would leave loud shadows, two families wondering what had happened to them. One person could go missing, have a breakdown, run away, but a young couple? No; people would suspect foul play, he would have to be clever, it was the ultimate test.

"They offer tours for small groups, transport, accommodation. I've done it before, if you're interested I can arrange it when the tour guide re-appears and let you know the itinerary later, even if you don't want to do it right now you'll have the details for when you're ready."

Brett took over the conversation, Jules happy to just smile and nod. "Yeah, we might be interested, I guess it wouldn't cost as much if we could go with a couple of others."

"Exactly and, it's always nice to have another English speaker along for company."

Jules squashed into Brett. "I think it sounds like fun, and it's always nicer to do things in a group."

Brett looked down at the brown eyes crinkling up at him, softening his male shell. "I guess so, we've got today to bum around together" he looked back to Matt "Okay mate, just give us a call later and let us know how you get on, room 233."

"Great." And Matt held his hand out to Brett, shaking the other man's hand enthusiastically. "I'll call you later."

Dirty Luggage

Matt stepped into the humid atmosphere of Bangkok, steam was rising from the large tropical banana palms that decorated the front of the hotel, honks and high pitched moped engines called him towards the city centre. He walked without seeing, his legs moving mechanically in an easy stroll, his mind unfurling, ideas skimming across his consciousness, conversations playing out inside him. In his pockets his hands were moving in response to his internal dialogue, his face occasionally frowning, smiling crookedly, a plan forming slowly.

A small park connected two of the main roads, a supposed pleasant area of green amongst the concrete filth of the city. His body turned the corner easily and his eyes re-focused on the green verges and tall palms. The park was surrounded by high rise apartments, washing hung out on drying racks cluttering the small balconies. A childrens playground was situated in the centre of a large green, the swings and climbing frame dotted with small brown bodies, their whoops and yells carried across the peaceful circle of the park. In a far corner two men lolled on the grass, their dirty brown faces creased into drunken wrinkles above clothes that seemed to be just hanging on to their wasted bodies. A young woman engineered her hips along the central path, her silver platform sandals bending her ankles precariously. As she passed Matt her shadowy eyes cast a flicker to his face, her pupils large and fixed, the dead mask of a drug addict. He sat down on a bench and took in the view of the whole sordid green circle. The desperately public lives of the people squashed into the tiny apartments, the children sharing a park with drunks and junkies, the risk of finding a disgusting needle. It just re-enforced Matt's view of the world. He did not fool himself, this planet was full of sad, dirty lives. Human beings were a damaged species, they were destroying the planet like they destroyed one another. Tragedy was always around the corner, you should never expect to be safe. Matt knew where the Fire Exit was in his hotel, he always knew how many rows he was from an exit on a plane, he wouldn't be surprised if one of the drunks stuck a knife at him as he walked past. There was little beauty left, he loved his family and that was it.

-19-

Jules loved Brett. She wound her arm around his as they walked back to the hotel, his brown muscles warm against her cheek, sometimes she wished she could disappear inside him. They had talked about children and he had, finally, said that he really wanted them. He said they should take it slowly, he wanted to complete his sabbatical first, a full lawyers wage should support them both allowing her to stay at home with the baby. She smiled to herself, of course she'd agreed. It would take her body several months to cleanse itself from the contraceptive pill and of course it would take several months after that to conceive. Well, that's what she told him but, secretly, she was hoping to fall pregnant straight away. It filled her heart to think she would be carrying his child, they would be a family, indelibly entwined. She squeezed his arm into her and gave a small skip, smiling at him she giggled "I love you" planting a kiss on his arm. Kissing her forehead he slipped his arm around her body and let his fingers tickle her right breast. Their bodies glued from shoulder to hip they squeaked across the marble floor to the lifts.

"I've really enjoyed today, it's been so nice just wandering round the shops with nothing to do. I think we should make the effort to go on that elephant trek before we go home, what do you think?" She rested her back on the cool chrome bar running round the interior of the lift.

"Hmmm, yeah, maybe that guy has left a message for us, I'll call reception when we get to the room."

"What did you think of the lovely Jerry?"

"Was he coming on to you before I came over?"

"No, of course not, he was just being friendly. I wouldn't be interested anyway stupid." She bumped her hip into the serious looking man beside her. Sometimes she wondered if he was a little too serious. "He was just saying he'd been here on business I think and how he'd done the trek before."

"Yeah, well, we can go ourselves anyway, if he hasn't called then we'll just crack on and book it anyway."

"Course, it's just I thought, if they put you in a group I would rather it was with a couple of English speakers we can have some fun with." The lift pinged to a halt and she stopped talking as they walked down the hushed and closed environment of the corridor. Someone had left a tray outside a door, the china plate speckled by black ants.

Jules felt clammy. "Phew, I'm gonna have a shower before dinner." Dumping her clothes on the floor she walked into the bathroom, her feet arching away from the cold tiles. Turning the tap on the wall, water began to jet from the shower nozzle in a soft, fine fizz. The contorted sounds of the television warbled through the spray to her ears. She looked down at her smooth, flat belly, the water meandering it's way around the contours and down between her legs. She touched her stomach and tried to imagine it swollen with a child inside, it would be so magical. The water was so soft it seemed to take forever to rinse the shampoo from her hair, the sea and sun damaged ends felt frazzled and knotted it cried out for conditioner. Twisting a towel around her wet hair and wrapping another around her body, she padded across the tiles and onto the hard, ridged carpet of the bedroom. A large presence seemed to cast a shadow into the room. In front of the patio doors and behind a small, curved armchair stood the Englishman, Jerry. She was so surprised to see him in their hotel room that, for a moment, her mouth hung open, no words were ready to respond. And then, with a sickening, freezing lurch, she realised Brett was unconscious. Slumped into the armchair, his head was hanging onto his chest. As her vision focused to gather more information she noted the way his arms seemed to be held behind his back with something, his legs spread unnaturally, his ankles attached to the chair legs with plastic twisty ties, like the handcuffs she knew air hostesses used. Her eyes moved slowly upwards from the top of Brett's head, over the pale blue cotton shirt of Jerry to his twisted grin. The face that had seemed so attractive this morning now had a coldness to it. The dark eyes staring with an evil that frightened her more than anything she had ever known. She wanted to scream but her larynx seemed to crack and a high pitched wail began to rise from her throat.

"*Shut the fuck up!*" Jerry's voice snapped across the room, sharp against the constant chatter of the television. She could see Brett's head begin to lift, a small groan that sounded like "Jules" trying to make itself heard. She stepped towards her husband, needing to comfort him, to hold him, make sure he was alright but as she made her first stride a crack sounded and Brett's body jerked upwards from the chair before his head dropped heavily onto his chest again. A small cry escaped her mouth as she noticed Jerry holding something to the back of Brett's head. At first she thought it was a gun but as her mind made more sense of it she realised the square box had two protruding horns, it was more like some kind of Taser or stun gun.

She forced herself to speak, her voice shaking with emotion, the sound almost alien to her racing mind. "What do you want?"

"I want you to listen to me very carefully and do exactly what I tell you. You're not going to scream, you're not going to try and alert anyone or your boyfriend won't wake up next time."

Her eyes were locked into his and she knew by the calm, cool way he spoke to her, that he wasn't bullshitting. "Okay, please don't hurt him. What do you want?" She was surprised how her voice had levelled out, a dormant instinct to survive had kicked in and her mind had slowed in concentration, trying to take in every detail. She just wished she could touch Brett though. Her chest felt like it was splitting in two, her heart breaking out of it's cage every time she looked down at her love's head dangling lifelessly.

"Firstly, I want you to get dressed." She was suddenly aware of her nakedness under the towel and was relieved to realise that he obviously wasn't going to rape her, it was the first time the thought had occurred. She looked on the floor at the crumpled clothing she had thrown down earlier. She didn't want to leave Brett and she didn't think this devil would allow her to dress in the bathroom anyway so she allowed the towel to drop as she struggled to pull her clothes on over her damp body. Her nudity exposed her and she felt the shakes begin to overtake her movements, her bottom lip quivering threateningly. She knew his eyes were on her the whole time, evaluating the wobble of her breasts and her exposed vagina. She did her best to turn slightly away from him as she lifted her arms to pull her t-shirt on. Standing straight on, her clothes creased and damp, she looked back at the powerful man that seemed to have taken control of their lives so suddenly. "Now, you're going to go back down to reception and tell them that you want to check out. Settle the bill and tell them you'll be leaving later tonight."

"What?" She couldn't help the question from popping out of her mouth. She was so confused, what the hell was this man doing to them.

"Just do what I fucking say."

"Okay." Jules turned to the hotel door, she wasn't sure how she was going to deal with this, at the moment she just felt like a robot being programmed by it's master.

"You'll need a credit card."

"Oh, yes." She turned back to the room. The top of the dressing table was covered in junk. Sunglasses, change, jewellery, deodorant, empty bottles of water. She pushed things around, the panic beginning to rise in her, surely she hadn't lost her purse? Her eyes finally landed on it, sitting obviously in the middle. She turned back to the door, scared to even look at Brett who she was sure was beginning to make tiny grunting sounds again.

"Oh, and Julie?"

She turned back to the mad Englishman.

"Don't try and get clever. If anyone finds out about this, if you speak to anyone, if that phone rings or someone else comes to that door, Brett will suffer." His hand was now on Brett's forehead, at some point he had dropped the stun gun. Brett's eyes were rolling around in their sockets, she could see he was searching for her, trying to fix on her shape. The Englishman then brought his other hand across Brett's throat, a silver blade pressed into his neck. He ran the knife across Brett's adam apple, slicing through the top layers of skin, a trickle of deep burgundy blood ran down his throat and spread along the seam at the top of his vest. "You see, they'll hang me anyway, so don't think I won't hesitate to kill him if you fuck around."

A sob choked Jules' throat, like a huge ball of cotton wool, she tried to talk through it "How do I know you won't kill him anyway?"

The Englishman fixed his dark eyes on her, his tone dropped, "I promise you" and he emphasised the word promise, "that if you do exactly as I say, you will find him alive and well when you get back to this room."

Turning the door handle down, the stupid fucking hotel signs falling across her knuckles, Jules swung the heavy door open. She half ran to the lifts in the centre of the corridor, clamping her hand across her mouth. Oh shit, what was she going to do? She shifted her weight from one foot to the other as the lift slowing pinged it's way up to her floor. She prayed to God there was no-one in the lift, the sight of another person would just break her and she was sure she would tell them. Would they even believe her? It was so absurd they'd probably just think she was a mad woman. The doors slid open and Jules stepped into the empty square. She jabbed her index finger into the G button and the doors closed swiftly. As it carried her to the Ground floor the image of Brett slumped on the chair sent her body into fine tremors. She couldn't risk that bastard doing anything to him, she couldn't risk letting anyone know. She'd check out and get back to the room as soon as possible then she could try and talk to him, do whatever he asked. It must be about money, there couldn't be anything else, she would help him get whatever he needed. He had seemed so pleasant this morning, there must be something wrong, he must need something desperately, she would help him and then he would leave them alone, after all, they didn't know anything about him, he could disappear easily afterwards, there was no need for him to do anything horrible.

The doors opened to a glittering foyer, the evening lights were on and they seemed to bounce off the polished marble floor, the brass railings and reflect off the crystal clear glass doors and windows. A murmur of voices was accompanied by the clatter of cutlery in the dining room off to her right. It seemed unbelievable that just this morning they had been sitting there having their breakfast.

Three people were standing in front of the reception desk, a man in a white shirt was talking to a smartly dressed woman, they looked like work colleagues. Behind them a small man, half bald was holding the handle of his suitcase, a heavy laptop bag dragged one shoulder down. The panic threatened to reveal itself, she wanted to scream at them, "Let me go first, I've got to save my husband" but she couldn't, they would know something was wrong. On the other hand, if she took too long, the Englishman might think she was up to something kill Brett and then walk away. Thankfully a second receptionist appeared from the office door and began to deal with the small balding man. The couple were saying thank you and moving to one side. Jules stepped forward and looked at the male receptionist. He seemed stressed and his polite "Can I help you madam?" held no real warmth or interest. His hair was black like Jerry's and his dark eyes were contorted by glasses. He looked like an Indian and she was grateful that their difference created a barrier that stopped her from breaking down.

"Yes, I'd like to settle my account please, we'll be leaving later tonight." She was conscious that her voice sounded unnaturally high pitched but he didn't seem to notice.

Walking back along the corridor to their room, the same prayer went round and round in Jules' head. Please let Brett be alright. She took a deep breath and knocked on the door. It opened immediately and she was looking straight along the length of the room to the balcony. The armchair was empty. Just as she stepped into the room, she noticed the bathroom door to her right was open, two feet were lying face down poking out of the doorway. The room door slammed shut behind her and she realised that the monster must have been standing beside it, concealed by the solid fire door the whole time. Fear, like the combination of all her nightmares, overtook her, a scream erupted from her shocked open mouth, as the sound pierced the air it became contorted by a crackling noise close to her left ear. It felt like a blow to the side of her head, it knocked the air from her lungs, the noise from the cavern of her mouth. Without closing her eyes the room became blackness and she was oblivious to the thump of her head hitting the wall.

It was hazy to start with, like trying to focus through soft gauze. She was conscious of a cracking, splitting headache, her arm went to rise instinctively to rub the painful spot but it couldn't move. Her heart beat in painful, racing pulses as she realised her wrists were clamped behind her back. She could feel the cool bathroom tiles against her right cheek, the flesh squashing her right nostril closed. Her vision was slowly clearing, the space directly in front of her eyes came sharply into focus. She was looking at the circular silver drain positioned in the floor of the bathroom, a rusty, red trail led from the drain to the bottom of a pair of sneakers. Following the legs upwards she could make out the back of Jerry's body leaning over the bath tub. His right arm seemed to be twisting and manoeuvring something, the veins on his left arm swollen with exertion as if it was holding a heavy weight. The underside of his shirt was covered in blood. She had to get out. Trussed up she began wriggling her way backwards out of the doorway, trying to control her noisy breathing. Her face began to scratch on the rough carpet of the bedroom, away from the bathroom she risked curling her legs up into the foetal position hoping to kneel. Using the room door for leverage she began to push her body up against it, the chrome door handle just inches away from her face. She could try pushing it down with her chin and then hopping round to the crack, using her face to edge the door open. A modern fire door, the handle squeaked with that awful springing noise as she pushed slowly down with her chin. Her eyes whipped round to the bathroom. Jerry's face was looking at her, anger flashing through the dark eyes, his mouth set in a furious snarl. His rough hand gripped her mouth, covering her nostrils, his whole strength dragging her back to the bathroom. Her face was looking directly up to the bright, white spotlights, blinding her, circles dancing in front of her eyes. And then a huge, dark shadow powered towards her, eclipsing her vision as the blinding pain of the mallet smashed into her face.

Matthew dragged the last suitcase into his room. It hadn't been easy, hot boning bodies was far more difficult, having to prepare a carcass within an hour of death was far harder than an animal that had been refrigerated overnight. He ran his finger along the edge of his knife. He was good. Even through all that work he'd kept it sharp, cutting through flesh like butter. He'd gotten so quick now, he could switch off from the whole process, they weren't people, just carcasses that need to be taken apart and disposed. Nothing left of them but plastic cards and bits of paper. It wasn't as if he even knew them, they were stupid enough to trust him, what did they expect? After cleaning up and changing he'd started to worry that the maid might arrive to service the room, he couldn't be sure how much time the girl had given him. He knew he was going to be too tired to get rid of the bodies tonight so he'd washed them well, clearing out the gut and bowels to reduce the smell in his room. He tipped his tools out into the bath, running the hot water until it covered them, they could soak overnight. The only thing that was pressing on his mind was the money. He needed to get on top of his paperwork, with so many passports and credit cards at his disposal he was keen to get spending.

Grabbing the notepad and pen beside the bed he started to practise the new signatures, the girl's was the hardest, loops and connections, the pen never seemed to leave the paper. He then pulled out the passport photos he kept in his wallet, carefully replacing the originals with his picture. He could even modify the girls passport, sticking an M over the F for female, the difference in male and female western names went above the heads of most of the Asians he met. If he dumped the bodies in the morning he would have the rest of the day for shopping and banking. His heart skipped a beat at the thought of his spending spree.

-20-

Everything was going well, Matt felt light in his heart as he heaved the two heavy bags onto the check in scales, even if they were overweight he didn't care, he had enough money not to worry about paying the excess. There were so many things he'd wanted to keep. He'd had to chuck the nice SCUBA bag, it stank so much that there was nothing he could squirt on it to disguise the smell. There was a really nice bag for Nieve, a sort of posh beach bag, very St. Tropez, hardly looked used, probably bought by the woman specially for that trip. She'd been wearing a Citizen watch, it was so pretty that he hoped Nieve would wear it. There were a couple of designer shirts he'd taken a fancy to, the same guy he'd gone diving with, he'd also had nice sunnies, perched on top of his head he fingered the PRADA logo. There were a few more odds and sods he hadn't had time to sort out yet, he knew his luggage was a bit of a state but he didn't really care. It wouldn't be long before he was a thousand miles away back home. He was flying to Singapore first, just for a day to finish some shopping, before grabbing a flight home to Mexico. He was looking forward to showing Nieve their bank balance, it was so healthy he could take some time off and work in the shop.

The check in girl handed him the passport and boarding card, she was obviously giving him a pass on the scales, he threw her a smile, throwing his small rucksack onto his back, he went in search of a mailbox, he wanted to send another postcard before heading to the departure lounge.

Sergeant Lee was on her hands and knees in the cramped space of the bathroom, in response to a call from her colleague searching the bedroom, she sat up, banging her head on the underside of the toilet. Rubbing the tender spot she joined Inspector Lowe.

"Just take a sniff in there" Lowe was holding the door to the wardrobe open. Lee stuck her head inside the heavy wood closet and breathed in, what had begun as a musty odour on the outside now became the rotting smell of animal juices.

"Oh god, that's disgusting." She pulled her head back, pinching her nose.

Lowe laughed. "Sorry, how you doing?"

"You need to have a look too, make sure I haven't missed anything." Lee led Lowe back into the white space of the bathroom. "See here," and she closed the door pointing to several small spots of blood, "and here, excuse me." She squeezed past her colleague, stepping into the bath tub she indicated the tiles behind the mixer tap. At the base, where a cleaner wouldn't ordinarily reach with a quick wipe, was a smear of coppery red.

"Ho, ho, ho, I reckon this is where he did it." Lowe lay on the floor, twisting his body round to gain a floorside view of the bathroom.

"Right, well there isn't room for both of us, I'm going to have a chat with reception and get this room sealed off." Lee stepped over the trim figure of her young colleague, collecting her pocket book and pen from the toilet seat.

She was too excited to take the elevator, favouring the sensation of running up the hotel stairs. Bursting into the room she found Lowe studying the carpet in the bedroom.

"I think we need to get scenes of crime in for that, their gear is gonna be a lot better than your nose!"

Lowe looked up sheepishly, his boyish smile under a flop of black shiny hair. "I know, I just thought we might get a head start."

"Well, they're on their way. Listen, I've been talking to the staff and it seems there was an Englishman in the room next door at the same time. No big deal except, these two were definitely seen arriving together, the bell hop remembers taking their bags from the same cab."

"Oh yes?" Lowe drew the words out with a hopeful inclination. "And where is said Englishman now?" His eyes rolled sideways to the partition wall, his voice lowering to a whisper.

"Oh no such luck, he checked out a week ago but," Lee dramatically pulled out a piece of paper from behind her back, "we know what he looks like as well as his name." Holding the paper between two fingers she positioned it in front of Lowe's face.

"Mr Jeremy Harwood." Standing up, Lowe took the paper.

"The hotel takes a quick photocopy of the guests' passports when they check in."

Back in the briefing room Lee pulled a chair up to the Super's desk.

"We need to speak to this guy" she slid the photocopy across. The Super pushed his spectacles up to the bridge of his nose as he studied the photograph. "Okay, I'll tell you what you need to do", easing the specs off, they dangled on the cord around his neck, "you need to speak to Sergeant Tan. He's been researching the transactions on Philip's credit cards since the expected time of death, you need to go and knock on some doors with this picture and see if it rings any bells. If it does, you might be on to something. You better both go, there could be a fair bit of statement writing."

The landline on the Super's desk trilled loudly, ignoring Lee, he picked it up. "Superintendent M speaking, oh hello," he placed his hand over the mouthpiece and mouthed America to Lee, he then held his thumb and little finger to his other ear mouthing 'Call Me'.

When the dark skinned Indian nodded recognition, Lee knew she was holding the picture of a killer in her hand. The manager of the World of Travel, didn't just recognise him, he remembered him distinctly. He'd been in and out several times, changing travellers cheques and transferring funds to an account in the States. The Manager had got involved when dealings with the dark-haired man had become too confrontational for the girls on the counters, he would not accept any delays necessary to clear funds.

It was time for Jeremy Harwood to be marked as wanted for questioning by the Singapore CID.

Matthew had enjoyed the flight. There was no work to think of, so he occupied himself with planning which shops he wanted to visit. He would spend some money on Philly, it was nice to spoil her, maybe she'd like some pretty dresses. He quite liked some of the Asian soft toys, impossibly large eyes, doleful, pandering to the most sentimental notions of animals, he would pick up something so large he had to carry it as hand luggage. She would notice it before she noticed her dad. He smiled, looking at the old lady next to him, there was something about feeling happy, it made him more sociable. She smiled in response and he took the opportunity to talk about his little girl, old people were always happy to listen to stories about children.

After a while he only noticed the woman's lips moving up and down. He couldn't be bothered to listen to her anymore, his eyes began wandering. A fine gold Timex watch sat on her wrist like a bracelet, her skin so thin that it rested on the little nuggets of bone at her wrist joints. Her hands rested on top of a paperback, the title caught his attention. It was a crime thriller.

"Are you enjoying it?"

The old lady seemed confused, she had been busy describing her home to him. "I'm sorry?"

"The book, are you enjoying it?"

She looked down at her lap, "oh, yes, I know it might seem a bit morbid but I do like something that makes you want to turn the page, I'm not really one for all that romantic rubbish."

Matthew was gazing at her hands again, distracted by the heavy jewelled rings, substantial gold they seemed from another era, she had obviously worn them for years, her fingers now too thin for them they had slid sideways with the weight of the stones. Her nails were smooth and strong, the cuticles still milky white, her hands remarkably soft, she was obviously well looked after.

Matt thought of the yellowing paperback in the hold above their heads. He had read it so many times it had become part of his consciousness, he had also learnt from it, it had been a point of reference for him for so long but now, he felt it's need lessening for him. He was a master at his crimes now, the book held nothing for him other than a memory of comfort when no-one understood him.

"I've got a book for you."

"Oh yes?" She didn't seem particularly interested but her good manners forced her to keep looking at the intense young man.

"It's in here somewhere." He stood up and clicked open the overhead locker, his height allowed him to reach inside with ease, none of that standing on tip toe that the hostesses needed to do. He pulled it from the rucksack.

"Here."

The old lady took the creased book, the jacket wanting to open of it's own accord. Matt sat back down, staring past her powdered face he seemed to be talking to the heavens outside the plane window.

"It's about a young boy. He has deep sadness in him, he's left in the care of his father whose a complete bastard. He ends up abandoned, hurt and lonely. In the end he finds great love."

The old lady frowned. "I'm not sure it's my cup of tea"

Matt continued, "you'll like it, he becomes a serial killer, not a cold hearted one though." He hastened to add, moving his eyes from the window to look at her face. "It's good, you'll enjoy it and you will even love him."

"Are you sure you want to give it to me, it seems to be a favourite of yours." She turned the book in her hand, noticing the number of pages that held the crease from the top corners being folded over.

"It's served it's time."

"Well, thank you, if you'll excuse me, I really want to try and finish this book of mine before we land." And she gave a small, closed lip smile as she picked up the book from her lap. Matt rested back in his seat, it was like the unburdening of something, a tiny piece of weight shifted onto someone else.

-21-

Matthew trailed along the rope that wound it's way towards the immigration desks. He was dying to phone Nieve, he couldn't wait to hear the pleasure in her voice when he told her he was coming home. The suitcase rolled effortlessly over the flat carpet but he felt awkward with a huge backpack weighing him down and his rucksack dangling from his arm. He supposed he could wrap it round his shoulders, opposite to the backpack wearing it across his chest, but somehow the look was just too 'studenty' for him and he put up with the shapeless bags lolloping and bumping into his body uncomfortably. He tried to ignore it, not wishing to ruin his mood, he felt tired but satisfied, tomorrow he would book a flight and then spend the rest of the time buying pressies.

He approached the officer's desk, handing over his passport with his free hand. Singapore airport was so efficient he was surprised when the large woman told him she was having a problem with her computer. He looked again at her face, it was too round, tiny spots across the bottom of her cheeks suggested a hormone problem or a weakness for greasy foods. She was staring at the concealed screen as if waiting for some sign. Matthew raised his eyes and surveyed the row of desks. A cold hand squeezed his heart, no-one else was kept waiting. Could it just be this computer? From the corner of his eye he caught the movement of two officers approaching the desks, Matthew fought to control the panic clawing inside his chest, raising his eyes to the bright lights he prayed that when he looked down again he would be greeted with the smiling face of the officer, holding out his passport and waving him through. His neck slowly straightened and his eyes grew level with the woman, she was looking straight past him, in his peripheral vision he felt the presence of the two officers standing either side of him.

He felt like a specimen in a tank. Glass ran from the ceiling to mid height, a panic strip running along the top of the lower half of the walls. He hadn't been handcuffed or anything but, sat on a chair fixed to the ground he felt completely powerless, as if his arms and legs had been chopped off. One of the immigration officers came into the room backwards, dragging the backpack and suitcase, the rucksack over his arm. Totally ignoring Matthew, he piled it all in the corner and left again. He sat in silence. The room was so well soundproofed that he couldn't hear anything from the open plan office surrounding him, he could see people talking, picking up telephones but not a sound reached him. He stared at the luggage in the corner. It had a life of it's own, even if he didn't say a word the luggage would tell the whole story. Documents, passports, bank cards, membership cards, drivers licenses, clothing, jewellery, cameras. The list went on and Matthew's head hurt as he tried to recall everything that might be in the bags. There were identities from America, Thailand, Singapore, he'd even kept the notepad he'd been practising signatures on. The green backpack seemed to be talking the loudest, the tools. He tried examining each one in his minds eye, how sufficiently clean were they?

Imperceptibly, Matthew began to rock, a dark presence was beginning to slither from his mind, it curled it's cold slimy body down into his chest, sucking the feeling from his heart, leaving a vacuous dark space inside Matt's head. It was telling him something, reminding him of something that he was refusing to acknowledge. As the tears began to prick his eyelids, Matt understood the message. This was Asia. They kill you for this. They would kill him for this. He would never see Nieve or his daughter again. The pain sliced into his heart, unconscious tears streamed down his cheeks as an animal rose inside him. He stood up from his chair and slammed his head into the glass window, the pain fulfilling the animal's anguish he smashed his head into the glass again and again until with a crack, the window splintered, crushed glass sticking to his wounded forehead. Three vicious looking shards had fallen onto the floor, Matthew picked one up, holding it so tightly that it cut the palm of his hand. He sliced it cleanly across his left wrist, the wound so sharp that it took a moment for the blood to rise from it. The door burst open and two officers charged towards him, one grabbed his arm fiercely, slamming it backwards onto the wall, the back of his hand bruised he dropped the glass shard. The other officer held his left wrist firmly, the blood running over his fingers.

Matt looked down at the top of their heads, his chest heaving with sobs that merged in and out of hysterical laughs.

"Lee!" The Supers voice flew across the office, causing other detectives to look up from their paperwork or frown into the telephone calls. Staff Sergeant Lee leaned round her monitor. "Yes sir?"

He was holding his mobile a few inches away from his face, a huge grin pushed his spectacles up on his round cheeks. "They've got your man at the airport."

Lee felt all of a flutter, unexpected arrests required planning, she liked to know her 'go bag' was well stocked with everything she could possibly need. The Super was one step ahead of her. "Crew up with Lowe, do the prelims at the airport, if you arrest him then bring him back to custody here."

"Okay sir." Lee pulled her jacket off the back of her chair and slung her equipment belt over her shoulder. "You ready?"

Inspector Lowe was tapping madly at his keyboard. "Yep, yep, let me just save this and I'm all yours."

The two officers jumped into the job car, Lowe taking the wheel allowing Lee to collect her thoughts. After ten minutes she delivered her pearl of wisdom. "Okay, I guess we just show up, have a look at him and go from there."

Lowe smiled. "That's just what I was thinking."

They streamed past the traffic on the highway, drivers taking offence to the unmarked vehicle overtaking everything it came up behind. Sweeping off the main road they turned onto the perimeter of the airport, slowing down whilst they agonised over road signs, trying to work out the closest position to the customs office. Eventually they approached the security gate that led into the inner workings of the terminal. Lowe opened his window and held his warrant card up for the gate officer to check. Taking no chances, the officer walked around to Lee's side and checked her card too. Returning to his small office he picked up the phone, Lee could see the man's expression softening towards them, finally putting the call down and directing them to the customs building.

Lee was surprised to see an ambulance parked across the entrance. Throwing a "what the hell?" face across to Lowe, they pulled open the doors. The van was empty, so too was the reception area. They made their way along the suspiciously quiet corridor until, the sound of raised voices pulled their attention towards an office on their right. Opening the door to a large open plan space, all the activity seemed to be centred on one corner. Two paramedics were administering to a tall, dark haired man, Jeremy Harwood. An immigration officer noticed the two detectives and walked over, holding his hand out and introducing himself.

"I'm afraid Mr Harwood decided to take justice into his own hands."

"Really?" Lee was more interested in the scene behind him and tried to step to the side for a better view.

"Yes, he's going to need to go to the hospital for a check up before he goes to the police station."

Lee looked to Lowe. "Not a problem, we'll grab all his property, I'll jump in the van and you follow okay?"

"Sure, let's bag and tag the luggage as it is and go through it back at the station. They're going to want to get a move on." Lowe indicated the paramedics.

Lee perched herself on the small platform in the back of the ambulance, gripping the edges as it cornered, her weight thrown from one side to the other. The man was just lying there, his eyes staring blankly above him, his mouth set in a straight line. As she began explaining his rights he turned away from her.

-22-

Guy walked into their cell, his clothes itched from trapped blades of grass and fragments of scratchy weed cuttings, he couldn't wait to strip off. Lesley was sat on his bed, his back leaning against the wall, his legs hanging over the edge. His nose was buried in the broadsheet, he managed a grunt in acknowledgement.

"Got your paper then?"

Another grunt. Guy eased his work boots off, using the toes of one against the heel of the other, he was too knackered to bend down. He gazed at the front page of Lesley's newspaper, a grainy black and white photograph caught his attention. Focusing on the image it seemed familiar, surely not, it couldn't be? He grabbed the paper from Lesley's loose hold.

"Hey, what the fuck are you doing?"

"It's him, jesus Christ it's him" under the headline banner 'The Tourist from Hell' a crazy and very broken looking Badger stared out at him.

"Who?"

"Hang on a minute mate." Guy sat on the end of the bed as he devoured the story, his gut slowly digesting the material and becoming increasingly sicker.

"Will you fucking explain you dick."

Guy lowered the paper and stared at Lesley. "It's Badger."

"The guy with the postcards?"

"Yeah."

"Shit man." He grabbed the paper back from the dazed Guy.

Lesley began muttering the story aloud. "He's been chopping people up all over the place, jees man the mother fucker's a complete nut." He looked up from the paper, staring at Guy like a stranger. "Did you know?"

Guy looked at the puzzled face of the round man, he couldn't believe he was serious. "Of course I didn't fucking know, what the fuck do you think I am." He stood up, running his hands in and out of his hair, tiny green specks of grass flicked over the cell. He walked slowly to one end of the small room and back again, his brain full of a million thoughts but unable to grab hold of a single one. He looked at the wall covered in girlie posters, prisoner artwork and photographs. The map.

"Oh my god, the map."

"What map?"

"There was a map. I was supposed to put the postcards on it, that was the whole idea of them. He had this map of the world on the cell wall, he'd stick notes all over it, they were his plans, he tried to tell me all about them but I didn't fucking listen, I didn't fucking listen, I just thought he was a bit crazy. He planned it all, he planned the whole fucking thing. Jesus Christ, it was in the book as well."

"What book?"

"His favourite book, I gave it to him. It was about a serial killer, he travelled all over the place, oh my god, it helped him didn't it?" Guy sank onto the bed, his head in his hands. "Oh mate, if I'd kept the map, if I'd kept the postcards then I could help, maybe I could help them find the victims or something."

Lesley felt for the anguished man sat beside him, he resembled a rung out tissue. "Hey, listen, the cops will be doing everything they can, a map and a few postcards isn't going to make a big difference, it's not like they held any real information. And as for the book, that's like the old arguments about music or computer games. It didn't turn him into anything, he was already like that."

Guy looked at his friend. "But the notes he stuck all over it might have meant something, I can't remember a bloody word of it now."

"Listen, listen to me. They've identified three of them, that's what he'll be tried for, they've got him."

Guy tried to imagine how the families felt when they looked at the picture of the man that had treated their loved ones with such brutality "but maybe there's others, at least it might help the families."

"Stop it, there's nothing you can do, your best off pretending it never existed in the first place, jeez what was the bloke trying to do to you anyway, make you a fucking accomplice?"

"You don't understand, you've got no idea. These bastards taught him how to chop people into pieces."

"What the fuck are you going on about now?"

Guy felt his voice rising but he needed to vent, it needed to come out. "He wanted to learn butchery, they put him on a fucking butchery course when he was inside."

"Well, they didn't know they were dealing with a fruitcake did they?" Lesley's voice was becoming even louder than usual, Guy's anger beginning to grate on his nerves.

"But they should know, they're the professionals, it's a *prison* for fucks sake, who the hell do you think is in here?"

Guy stood up, his anger was like burning fuel in his limbs. Lesley mirrored his actions, both men standing in the small space less than a metre from one another.

"I think you need to get a grip mate, you're right, you are in a fucking prison, who did you think you were going to meet in here?"

Guy looked into Lesley, the normal jovial face was white, a nasty glint in his eye's, the cold criminal, the reality of the man.

Guy had to get away, his senses were pounding against the four claustrophobic four walls "I'm going to the gym."

He blindly walked through the prison grounds to the recreation area, ignoring all greetings from other inmates. There was only one other fella in the gym, so broad he was like a side of meat, his upper body so overdeveloped that his legs looked like forgotten spindles. He was pumping out bicep curls in front of the mirror, a roar escaping his throat as he came to the end of each set. Guy jumped on the treadmill, keeping his finger on the speed button until his legs thumped so quickly that he almost struggled to keep up. His breath began to hurt as his chest heaved to pump oxygen around his demanding limbs. This wasn't enough. He slammed the stop button and his legs heavily fell to dropped to a standstill. Walking over to the corner he fished out a pair of boxing gloves from the plastic equipment boxes. Approaching the punch bag he sank his fist into the canvas. The bag hardly moved but moulded satisfyingly to the shape of his fist. He thumped it again until his muscles had prepared themselves for the exercise. He threw a round of crosses in before tucking his elbows into his sides and firing out uppercuts, his knuckles ricocheting off the bag and he dug deeper, fighting hard to make an impression. Standing back he then sent his arms into a fast cycle of jabs, his limbs sprinting until the lactic acid built to a painful level and he had to let his numb arms drop to his sides.

"Anger and floppy hair just don't seem to go together."

Guy looked to the origin of the voice, the heavy weight lifter was looking at him in the mirror. Guy noticed how shiny his bald head was, smooth until it fell down the back of his neck where two tight rolls sandwiched on top of one another. Guy felt the tickle of sweat trickling down the sides of his face, his fringe stuck to his forehead blocking any chance of a breeze.

"You're right mate, have you got any clippers?"

"Course, give me ten minutes and I'll sort you out."

Guy watched the heavy locks fall on the floor around the chair, they seemed to land in curves, dark 'C's scattered over the felt carpet. It was like peeling off a layer, no more fucking pretending, no more everything's just fine and dandy. He was sick of fighting the depression, sick of guarding against the effects of prison life. It *had* changed him, it *had* been the worst, most fucking awful time of his life. He would never be the same person again. He'd intended to keep the act up when he joined his old social circle afterwards, play the ever happy, ever chilled Guy Hudson. Not now, fuck them, he was different, his heart was harder and he was not going to deny it any longer. He'd lost something, innocence or naivety or faith. Look at who he was friends with now, this is who he was. This was what he was. He looked in the mirror, his skull was grey, his hair had spent years cloaking it from the sun, his temples were bony and cavernous, his cheek and jaw bones more prominent. His face seemed harder, older; good, that's how he felt inside.

Walking back to the cell his chin was raised a little higher than usual, his arms swung loosely and his hips rolled ahead of him. He passed a junkie, bitter and vile, known for sticking pointy little knives into people.

"Fuck me, nancy boy's got a haircut." Guy stopped, turning round he looked at the vicious face, a smug smile, taunting. He stepped closer, breaking the personal space of the wiry weasel. His right arm propelled in front of him, grabbing the weasel round his throat, the force pushing him against the wall. Now Guy could feel all his training kicking in, his muscles now had a purpose. "What did you say?"

A flicker of uncertainty crossed the weasel's face but he was comfortable in the knowledge that he was not staring into the eyes of a known violent man. His throat was beginning to constrict, words would be difficult to form, a growl vibrated in his throat and with a pop of air he spat into Guy's face. The saliva ran down Guy's nose, crawling closer to his lips, his skin reeled in disgust. He dropped his right arm from the straining neck, looking away briefly before raising his shoulder, drawing on all the angry strength in his body, he pounded his fist into the lean man's face. A blindess came over him, the stinging pain in his hands was not satisfying enough, his fists began to pulverise into any soft part of the doubled up man he could connect with, the blows sending shocks down his body that ran back up through his arm's ready to fire into the disgusting piece of shit in front of him. He hated him, he hated everything he stood for and he hated him most for reminding him of what he was. The white blindness had deafened him, the siren was reeling around the corridor as his legs began to plant kicks into the curled up man on the floor in front of him. Arms smothered him, around his neck, vice like grips on his wrists, the unforgiving metal of cuffs slammed onto his adrenalin pumped veins. His head hit the floor, his cheek squashed so that the air struggled to breathe smoothly in and out of him, he was facing the crumpled weasel, trails of blood ran across his face, black streams from his nose, bubbling out of his mouth, tiny flecks scarlet red on the whitewashed wall.

Guy felt a wave of calm relax his trussed up body, his hands were beginning to throb but the pain was like a tonic, a physical sensation that connected with the drama he felt inside.

-23-

Nieve, Mexico

Nieve picked the envelope up from the scratchy rattan door mat. So this was it then, the explanation. Why he hadn't returned, why she'd had to give up the lease on the shop space, why the landlord was now on her back for the rent. She looked at the childish scrawl on the envelope, she knew what it was going to say. Deep in her heart she'd always known that he would end up getting arrested again, the leopard that couldn't change his spots. How she'd wanted to believe it would be different this time but there was no realistic way that Matty could earn good money without crossing those boundaries. Kids tele blinked and coloured the sitting room, Philly entranced by the flickering square box. Nieve took the letter and sat in the shade of the courtyard. The distant traffic rolled like the sea, notes of vehicles along the road outside rising up and down. Sitting on the stone wall she slid her thumb along the gummed triangle and pulled out the thin sheets of note paper.

Time stood still, the world grew silent as the words lifted from the page. After reading it twice she lowered the paper, like a tablet of doom, onto her lap. The sky was sapphire blue, the green of the fig leaves translucent as the white hot sun crossed the centre of the courtyard. The beats of the cicadas rose in symphony with the blind heat. The smallest sounds seemed amplified to Nieve's shocked senses, the scuttle of a shiny skinned lizard through the crisp undergrowth behind her, the air beating flap of a birds wings as it stretched itself in the tree above, preparing for the hottest part of the day. The pad of her daughter's running footsteps as she crossed the kitchen floor.

"Mama?" she knew she couldn't see her, tucked into the darkest corner of the courtyard.

"Mama?"

"I'm here." The little girl screwed her eyes up as she looked into the space outside, the light in stark contrast to the dim, cool interior. Philly spied the letter in her mother's lap, walking across, her greedy hands ready to grab it.

"Is it daddy?"

Nieve snatched the paper up and crushed it back into it's envelope. "No my precious one, it's not your father"

"Oh, who is it?"

"It's Matthew."

She could see the confusion running like a wave across her daughters' mind, the questions forming like the surf behind her eyes. "But.."

"No darling, your father is in England"

"Is Matthew coming home?"

"No darling, he's got to work away now. We won't be seeing him again"

"Oh."

Nieve knew that Philly would be asking more. Her mind would digest what her mother had told her and would not be satisfied, it knew there were holes, but for now, she would have to wait, Nieve wasn't ready to offer anything more.

"Come, it's time for a rest, lie down with me Philly, we'll sleep in your room."

Nieve felt the soft exhalations of Philly's breath tickling the hair on her arm. She didn't know what the future now held for her or her daughter, it was like staring down a lens that had been painted black. She had loved this house, it's high ceilings, the beautiful polished floors, but now it held something sinister, even if she could have afforded it she would not stay. Matthew needed to become a distant memory to her daughter, she could not bear to think of the dark soul that had been such a huge presence in their lives. She would pack the essentials and leave the rest. Let the landlord do what he wanted with it, maybe it was time to build some bridges and look for sanctuary with her family. Life needed to feel normal, Philly could get to know her cousins, Nieve would need to share this horrifying news with her family, this would not remain a secret for very long and she couldn't deal with it on her own.

She tried to picture the man she loved sitting in his cell, his whole life behind him. Why had he done it? Now he had made her feel dirty for loving him, for caring about him because whatever he had done, she couldn't just forget what he had been to her.

-24-

Matthew, Singapore 1996

He'd adjusted to his cell, the straw mattress that poked through his bed blanket, the flies that hovered over his toilet hole, bumping blindly into him as he stood in the eight by six space. They'd given him a television, sometimes he'd leave it on all day, the sound of other human voices, their banal conversations, their meaningless lives played out in front of him. It was like a small stage in the vacuum of his existence, soap operas, news bulletins, daytime chat shows, everyone fooling themselves that somehow it mattered. This petty existence, like ants scurrying around believing they were giants. When the sun was at a particular angle, rays filtered into the gloom, like golden messengers, they were a sign from up above, a reminder that he was not forgotten.

At first he'd felt angry, why had God abandoned him? He knew what was in his soul and yet he was allowing the powers on this world to punish him. He thought he should fight them, make them see that they had made an error, they couldn't kill him for this, it wasn't him. But slowly, as the empty space had dripped into him, filling the dark well inside, he realised that this was his destiny. He was too much for this world, it had never understood him.

Some days he stayed silent. Not one word, no solitary note would escape his lips, the dry, cracked skin would scratch together all day long, parting occasionally for food or liquid. Other days, the door would open and someone would step in, like the priest. He could talk to him. Sometimes he would touch his hands, look straight into his eyes, there weren't many people that would do that nowadays. The officers that worked here knew what awaited you, they saw it week after week. There was nothing to be gained by making a connection with the prisoners in this wing. The priest offered comfort, he had such beautiful English.

"For if you forgive men their trespasses, your heavenly Father will also forgive you. But if you do not forgive men their trespasses, neither will your Father forgive your trespasses."

Matthew understood that, he didn't blame them. He liked to write. One day they would read it and understand that they had killed something beautiful, they had taken Gods role and they would have to face the consequences when their own time came.

There were things he still didn't understand. He couldn't remember mutilating the bodies. He had only taken them to pieces, or so he remembered. Sitting in the court room he had placed his head in his hands as he tried to bring forth the memories, they said he had cut the man's dick off. He could picture the body, the white skin, slightly loose, probably from sitting in an office too much. He remembered the pubic hair, it had brushed softly against the back of his hand as he'd worked at the hip joints. He couldn't remember the penis. Was it big, small? There was a small growl inside him, the dark creature that liked to scratch at his consciousness sometimes, he knew it was trying to tell him something but he couldn't find it, didn't want to find it. It had made him angry in court, it was like they were accusing him of something, like a fucking homosexual. He knew he wasn't that.

The anger had lived inside him for the first couple of months. It had simmered in his veins, kept him awake at night, pushed his mind against the confines of his cell. Then, slowly, the truth had grown, like a wall, one brick every day until it rose, impenetrable, undeniable. He would die. If he fought the truth he might succeed in prolonging it but eventually it would happen. The anger had subsided and like the washed up debris from a great storm, he was left with himself and what remained of his human existence.

Exhaustion dragged down every cell of his body. He lay on his straw mat, the sick feeling inside him rising. Closing his eyes he hoped sleep would come, soothing his tired mind and dispersing the sickness. What was the darkness in him that separated him from everyone else? Had he been born with it? It was all he could remember. He knew his mother didn't have it, she was strong and warm, as a small boy he had only ever wanted to be held in those large feminine arms, the smell of cigarettes and cheap perfume overcoming his senses. He had never really known his father. He knew there had been some connection. The travelling, the constant need to move, was that his father's legacy? Long road trips sat in the front of his father's lorry, the endless grey of concrete motorways, road signs in foreign languages flashing in front of him before whipping past, already a memory. And the darkness that slowly grew in the evenings, the road lights twinkling in the dusk, an orange glow that would stripe the cab as they passed one after another all spaced equally.

He loved the curtains that turned the vehicle into a den. Curling up on the large bench that ran behind the drivers seat, he felt like a mouse snug inside a burrow. And then there was worry, an insecurity, was his dad leaving him alone? He sat up and peeked underneath the beige curtains. They were parked in a layby, dark woodland behind. The trees like a fortress, a spiky dense world of imagination, monsters from fairytales, bears, owls with sharp white faces. From the darkness the pale face of a man stepped out. Matthew ducked lower, wanting to watch without being seen. The man was thin, his body in shadow, only his face and hands visible, hands that were zipping up the fly on his trousers. He looked around before disappearing into a transit van. Matthew continued to look into the black hole in the trees. A larger figure appeared, his dad. He was looking straight at the cab. Matthew lay back down quickly, closing his eyes and trying to calm his breathing. He heard the creak of his dad's door opening and the gentle rock as he heaved his heavy weight up into the truck. Matthew knew his father was looking at him, he could feel his presence leaning over the front seat, almost detect his breath passing over his face.

He talked to the Priest about it. There was no comfort this time. "'Do not practice homosexuality, having sex with another man as with a woman. It is a detestable sin', Leviticus 18:22."

A mosquito woke him up, it's hum like the whine of a small fighter plane. He didn't have long left now. The thought sent a bullet into his stomach, he breathed out, capturing the calm and shattering the bullet into a thousand tiny, insignificant pieces. Philly came to him, her brown eyes questioning, searching his for understanding. She was his legacy, in her he would always breathe. She had a pure heart, they would not judge her. He hoped she would remember him, he would be waiting for her when her time came. And Nieve, she would know he was there for her. They would be able to live freely, their love entwining them eternally.

The priest was coming again this morning, he knew he liked talking to Matthew, he could tell him things, he was so close to the other world that he almost inhabited it. And the priest would be there at the end, he would watch as Matthew accepted his fate calmly, letting go of this painful existence, stepping into a world that welcomed him, loved him.

It was the last time he would see his mother. He was angry that they had not taken the leg irons off, that she had to watch him shuffle into the room like an animal in chains. He felt like a great bear, reduced to half starvation, performing tricks for a few scraps. There was a table between them, they were not allowed to touch. He wondered why, did they think he could capture some of her spirit, take her with him or, was it just that human touch could connect people as no other thing could. The pain of it would be too much to bear.

She was trying not to cry. Her lips were tightly pursed, she was not going to let these bastards take her dignity as well as her son.

"It's okay mum, I'm ready."

A tear escaped, it's soft, round emotion ran over the curve of her cheek and landed on the cream blouse.

"It's not right, it's not right." She stopped herself, her voice was cracking dangerously.

"It's what God wants, he's sending them a message, he'll look after me."

Her hands were screwed so tightly the nails were digging half moon shapes into the fatty flesh of her palms. She was looking at the floor, he knew she was looking to be anywhere but in this room.

"I want to know about Dad, mum."

She looked up sharply.

"Why did he kill himself?"

"I don't know son." But she didn't meet his eyes.

"Was he like me?"

And now she did look at him. "Sometimes I think you must be like your father, all this," she cast her eyes around the concrete room, "you certainly didn't get *this* from me, but maybe," she hesitated, "your dad messed with your head." Her cheeks flushed. "I'm not saying that I knew what was going on with your dad, I'm just saying that 'e was messed up an' he couldn't live with 'imself."

Matthew knew there was something in what she *wasn't* saying, but he didn't press her, it was all too late.

They didn't have long, the visit was ended abruptly. Probably on purpose, no-one ever wanted to say goodbye, not the ones left behind anyway.

The night was heavy. He moved his mat so that he was looking straight up, out of the small square window. The stars were tiny sparkles on a black velvet cape. He remembered the hero in his favourite book, his doppelganger. He had been saved from the gallows by his love. Rescued in a last minute twist of fate, his heart rejoicing that she still loved him. He had not been betrayed, he could still have faith in the soul of the one woman he had chosen to give his heart. But just as the tears of joy had tumbled from Matthew's eyes, spreading across the page, the bitter blow. It had been a double cross, the whore killed him herself. Matthew knew not to believe anyone would be there to rescue him, there would be no last minute reprieve, instead he would like to take the power from their hands. Tie the knot himself, wrap the rope tightly around his neck, feel the squeeze against his throat, the air unable to escape, unable to inhale. He would keep his eyes open, stare at them while he killed himself.

Three thirty in the morning, time had run out. The two officers lead him from the cell along the corridor. Their footsteps echo on the concrete floor. There is no other sound, the prison is still sleeping. Two other men are in the waiting room. Eyes like rats, cornered, looking down the barrel of a shotgun. The hangman talks in whispers. Each of them takes a turn to stand on the scales. He notes their particulars, calculating the length of each rope needed. They sit quietly in a row on a bench. The man furthest from Matthew is sobbing silently, a sound no-one is acknowledging. He can feel the shakes from the man beside him, fine tremors that run from his arm into Matthews.

The dawn is beginning to break, blue light begins to penetrate the cracks and openings in the prison. A black hood is placed over Matthew's head. The fabric is coarse, musty, his breath bounces back at him, condensing into a wet patch that irritates his chin. He recognises the voice of the Priest, "Yea, though I walk through the valley of the shadow of death, I will fear no evil; For You are with me; Your rod and Your staff, they comfort me..." But there is a verse that is even louder in Matthew's head, one that he read and wished he hadn't, "But the fearful, and unbelieving, and the abominable, and murderers, and whoremongers, and sorcerers, and idolaters, and all liars, shall have their part in the lake which burneth with fire and brimstone: which is the second death." Words he cannot forget. And the nightmare that has haunted him for so long begins to appear inside the claustrophobic world of Matt's new consciousness. There is a face, it's lips swollen and purple, and round it's neck, embedded into the flesh is electrical cable, and it's feet swing backwards and forwards like the pendulum of a clock. Sweat itches his forehead, there is no air inside the mask, he begins to pant, like an over exerted dog, his eyes dart from side to side, please god let there be some light, a crack, a shadow, anything but this blindness. His heart is racing like a tram scudding lightly across a track, his chest heaving up and down as he desperately tries to find oxygen. His arms strain against the binds on his wrists, like an animal in a slaughter house. His palms slippery with cold sweat, his bladder tickles; the fear of losing control sends another wave over his palpitating heart. His feet hit a step, he stumbles onto the wooden platform. He wants to scream, he is screaming but no sound escapes. The weight of a rope lands on his collar bone, there is a whipping sound as it is tightened. Voices, foreigners, colleagues; another days work. Do they see the trembling man in front of them? Have they noticed the dark stain spreading on his trousers? Please God, someone save him. Hush, sudden silence; and a crack as the floor disappears from under him.

-25-

Guy

People said hello to him as he walked along the landing, old inmates that recognised him, familiar faces like walking into a pub in the town you grew up in. Guy followed the screw, the jangle of his keys accompanying every step along the iron grill.

"Here you go mate." And he stood aside, allowing Guy to enter his new home. Standing in the centre of the cell was a slim, bearded man. Probably only thirty something, Guy could see the lean contours of his face above the curly dark mane of hair. His eyes glinted, clean and sharp, there was no trace of the clouds that shadowed the junkies faces.

"Hello, I am Kershnik, please call me Nik." He extended his hand to Guy, the muscles on his forearm clearly defined, the veins thick and healthy.

"Guy."

"Pleased to meet you Guy, you have the top bunk okay?"

"Sure." Guy threw his kit onto the thin mattress. So, here he was again but, this time, it felt different; comfortable, the small bricks in the wall had a familiarity about them, his nose recognised all the elements of the smell of enclosed men, he knew how to speak their language, his defences were always raised, his shell hardened, the core of himself locked away. A new cellmate to share some time with, another personality crossing his path, a live-in partner, a close relationship and then, just as suddenly as they were thrown together, one would leave and they would probably never see each other again. He looked at the smart man watching him, his beard was long, like a Muslim, but his complexion was fairer, like a European.

"Where are you from Nik?"

"Albania but I have lived many countries. My wife and baby are back there now and I join them soon," he smiled, shrugging his shoulders, "I hope." Guy began to notice the luxury items around the cell, the bottom bunk had a headboard and two mattresses. Behind the cans of deodorants and shaving foams on the desk a small collection of herbs and spices in cooking jars.

"Here, I show photographs." And the Albanian's arm moved swiftly behind him, pulling out the drawer of the desk together with a quick bang in the back corner. A piece of MDF fell flat in the drawer, the exact size of the back board. He picked up a mobile phone, his dexterous thumb pressing the buttons until he held the small screen in front of Guy's face. A picture of a young woman bending her head into the blonde curls of a little girl.

"Very sweet."

"Well, I must leave you, I have some business to do." He flicked the phone to the back of the drawer and pushed the board over the top. Closing the drawer he then pulled off the false front and withdrew a tobacco pouch from between the two pieces of wood.

"I see you later Guy." And with a smile, his lips concealed by the curly beard, he was gone.

Pulling his kit bag open he pulled out the post the office had given him. A couple of letters from mum, one from Gina and a postcard, a cityscape of Bangkok. Guy stared at the glossy photograph, did he send them before of after he killed someone? He knew from the newspapers that he was sentenced to death, was he gone yet? Turning the picture over he looked at the childish scrawl, it had been written some time ago, it must have been stuck in the prison postal system, chasing him between institutions. He ran his fingers over the ink, was there still blood on his hands as he held the pen? It struck Guy that no emotion had attached itself to the postcard. The sick anger that he had first felt had dissipated, a cool, dispassionate eye now gazed at the colourful lights glittering from the high rise offices. He propped it up against the wall behind the desk, he would consider it a bizarre memento from someone who had looked to him for friendship.

It was time to call his parents, it was now while the door was open or he'd be putting it off another twenty four hours. He slipped the phone card into the pocket of his trousers and stepped onto the landing. His eyes looked along the balcony and across the drop to the landing the other side. A skinny bloke with a greasy pony tail was curled into the phone box to his right, to his left three old lags were crowded around a cell door, like old men passing the time of day, roll ups sticking to their mouths or pinched between yellow fingers. Guy decided they looked harmless enough and risked squeezing past them to the call box.

"Alright posh boy, what you doing back 'ere?" Guy stopped in his tracks, the voice had boomed out from within the crowded cell, he recognised the gravely tones of the Slasher. Looking in he could see the large figure sitting on the bottom bunk, holding court amongst the brainless idiots who worshipped him with their sycophantic fear.

"Didn't think anyone'd recognise ya did ya, *ha* you can't fool me"

"Alright mate, how you doing?"

"I'm good, it's all good. You off to make one of your phone calls? I'd like a bit of a hand up as well if you're on it."

"Sorry mate, that's why I'm back here. It's all gone wrong."

"Oh, that's a terrible shame mate, we'll have to find you some other kind of work then won't we?"

"I guess so, cheers mate, I'll speak to you later" Guy continued walking towards the phone, thankfully the voice didn't follow him. He'd have to deal with it later, it wasn't going to go away.

With each ring of the handset, Guy's heart jumped in his throat, his mouth was so dry he wasn't sure any words were going to make it at all.

"Hello?"

"Hello mum, it's Guy."

"Guy, we haven't heard from you for ages, what's happened?"

"I'm back at the old prison, things went a bit wrong for me."

"Oh." And he could just picture her, the blue eyes filling as the emotion threatened to overtake the conversation. He knew she would be sitting down on the chair beside the phone in the hallway. She wouldn't want to be thinking about her legs, concentrating her energy on keeping herself together, trying to gather information she could regurgitate to dad later.

"What happened?", Her voice neither rose nor fell.

"I got into a fight mum, I'm sorry."

"Guy" Her tone was incredulous. "You've never been a fighter."

"I know, it's this place mum, it does something to you. I've tried so hard not to let it but it creeps up on you, you don't want it to. It's hard not to let the place influence you, it's all you see, all you hear, all you're surrounded by. You can't expect to live in these places and come out untouched."

"But Guy, you've never been one for violence. I know your dad goes on at you but that's for silly stuff, not thinking, you know," her voice began to break and the words squeaked breathlessly from her, "please don't tell me you've changed, please don't change, don't become like one of them, you're not like them." And she broke off, her sobs taking over the ear piece.

"Mum, they're just people, people like you and me. Life has just dealt them different cards. You can't say that any one of us would have been any different if we had lived the same life. I'm no different to anyone else in here, can't you see that. This has been my life for so long now." her sobs continued, there was nothing he was willing to say to make it any easier for her. "Look mum, talk to dad, let him know what's happened. I'll call you again soon, try and arrange a visit, please mum."

"Mm hmm." And he could see the tears running over her lips, taste the salt as she tried to open her mouth to speak. "I love you darling."

"Love you too mum." And he slowly placed the handset on the receiver. Somehow the slow click didn't feel enough. He picked the handset up again and smashed it back onto it's cradle. It wasn't enough. He held the handset by the mouthpiece and smashed the earpiece against the wall, the plastic splitting exposing the metal guts of the phone. Painful fingers sank into his biceps yanking his arms roughly behind him, metal cuffs cutting into his wrists.

"Down to solitary mate." And the two screws dragged him along the landing.

Guy lay on the bare concrete floor. His stomach was empty but he didn't want to eat. His mouth was dry but he didn't want to drink. His eyes were exhausted, stinging in the darkness, but sleep wouldn't come. His dreams played themselves out on the black canvas in front of him, dancing lights, shapes like clouds moving across the sky, as he tried to capture one it would transform into another. His tongue pressed against his back teeth, his jaw so tense that it threatened to bite down on it. The metal hatch on the cell door slid open.

"You want some scram mate?"

It felt so good to release some anger into the blank space around him, the growl began in the pit of his stomach, it clawed his insides as it built it's strength, moving faster and faster until it reached his mouth. He let it stretch itself open, roaring into the darkness.

"*No, fuck off!*"

Printed in Dunstable, United Kingdom